A Guide to

THE CONSUMER
PROTECTION ACT 1987

Preface

The Consumer Protection Act 1987 is perhaps the most wide-ranging piece of consumer protection legislation ever to have passed into English law. It has three main purposes. First, the Act provides consumers with a strict liability remedy against a producer whose defective products cause personal injury or damage to property: this is in line with the EEC's Product Liability Directive, published in July 1985. Secondly, it creates the offence of supplying goods which contravene a new general safety standard, the 'general safety requirement'. Thirdly, the Act repeals the troublesome section 11 of the Trade Descriptions Act 1968, and provides for the removal of the incomprehensible Price Marking (Bargain Offers) Order 1979, replacing them with the more comprehensive offences of giving to consumers a misleading price indication and of failing to correct a price indication which has become misleading. The opportunity has also been taken to consolidate, with some amendments, earlier legislation authorising the making of safety regulations for specific classes of goods, and to extend and unify the powers of enforcement authorities. It may be seen that the Act has significant implications for manufacturers, distributors, retailers and consumers alike.

The Act received the Royal Assent on 15 May 1987 and was, along with a number of other pieces of 'non-party' legislation, saved from being lost on the dissolution of Parliament by being pushed through its outstanding parliamentary stages in a matter of days. The Consumer Protection Bill had originally been introduced in the House of Lords and, by the date of the announcement of general election, had passed the Lords and had received its Second Reading in the Commons. In the following frantic week the Bill was rushed, virtually undebated but nevertheless amended in some significant respects by the government, through the Commons, and their Lordships became faced with the choice of opposing those amendments and thereby killing off the Bill, or of accepting them under some degree of protest. This book testifies to their choice of the latter option. The Act is due to come into force in the Autumn of 1987.

I owe thanks to Lord Hacking, a partner in the Litigation Department of Richards Butler, who throughout the passage of the Bill made sure that I received all relevant parliamentary materials as soon as they became available. His own contribution to the Bill in the

Lords' debates itself proved to be significant. Heather and Uschi of Financial Training have done a remarkable technical job in producing a book so speedily, despite having been unsure as to whether this particular phoenix would be rising from the ashes of a dying Parliament (or indeed what size or shape of phoenix it would be) literally until the day of Royal Assent. Thanks also to Barbara, my wife, for her continuing support and for restraining my daughters Eleanor and Lucy from putting into practice their various youthful suggestions as to alternative uses for an unguarded manuscript.

Robert Merkin
June 1987

Chapter 1

Background to the Product Liability Provisions

1.1 Pre-Existing Law

Liability in England for injury or damage to persons or property, caused by defective products, was, before the passing of the Consumer Protection Act 1987, somewhat haphazard and arbitrary. The rules governing liability remain in force after the Consumer Protection Act 1987, but the Act will generally provide a superior remedy. Two classes of person potentially face liability under the pre-existing law: the manufacturer of the product, in tort; and its ultimate commercial seller, in contract.

1.1.1 Position of the manufacturer

The landmark decision on the liability of the manufacturer to the person ultimately suffering loss was *Donoghue* v *Stevenson* [1932] AC 562 in which the duty of the manufacturer was set out by Lord Atkin, at p. 599, in the following terms:

> . . . a manufacturer of products, which he sells in such a form as to show that he intends them to reach the ultimate consumer in the form in which they left him with no reasonable possibility of intermediate examination, and with the knowledge that the absence of reasonable care in the preparation or putting up of the products will result in an injury to the consumer's life or property, owes a duty to the consumer to take that reasonable care.

The duty does not, however, extend to two important forms of loss: damage to, or diminution in the value of, the defective product itself, and to any property damage to which could not be foreseen (*Aswan Engineering Establishment Co.* v *Lupdine Ltd* [1987] 1 All ER 135); and pure financial loss, such as loss of profits flowing from a defect in machinery, unless that loss flows from damage caused by the defective product to other property (*Muirhead* v *Industrial Tank Specialities Ltd* [1985] 3 All ER 705).

The difficulty for a victim in establishing a cause of action at common law has proved not to be in demonstrating the existence of a duty of care towards him, but in demonstrating both that there had been a breach of duty by the manufacturer and that the breach had in fact caused his loss. In *Daniels* v *R. White & Sons Ltd* [1938] 4 All ER 258 the plaintiff's claim against a manufacturer, for personal injury caused by carbolic acid contained in a bottle of lemonade, failed as she had not been able to establish that there was any point in the manufacturer's process at which negligence by the manufacturer could have led to the introduction of the acid into the bottle. A later decision, *Hill* v *James Crowe (Cases) Ltd* [1978] 1 All ER 812, took a more generous approach to the victim and imposed upon the manufacturer the burden of disproving the prima facie assumption that there had been negligence, but the conflict between the decisions still awaits final resolution. The causation question raises equal difficulty for a plaintiff, for even if breach of duty by a manufacturer can be shown, the suggestion by the manufacturer of some other equally plausible reason for the victim's loss will be fatal to the claim; for an illustration, see *Evans* v *Triplex Safety Glass Co. Ltd* [1936] 1 All ER 283.

These factors combine to make common law negligence litigation in respect of defective products both expensive and protracted. Where the product in question is sophisticated or the result of detailed research, the court will often be faced with competing evidence about the state of technical knowledge, the adequacy of precautions and the cost of incorporating safety features into the product; the evidence presented in *Vacwell Engineering Co. Ltd* v *BDH Chemicals Ltd* [1971] 1 QB 88 demonstrates this problem.

It had long been clear that the fault system of compensation for the victims of defective products, resting on proof of negligence, was unsatisfactory. The detailed study of the Royal Commission on Civil Liability and Compensation for Personal Injury (the Pearson Commission, Cmnd 7054), which was published in 1978, confirmed, at least in the context of personal injuries, that compensation to those most severely injured was frequently unobtainable and was often inadequate where it was obtained. The solution suggested by the Commission was a system of strict liability, i.e., compensation from the manufacturer without proof of any fault on his part.

1.1.2 Position of the retailer

In many cases the deficiencies of the law of negligence can be overcome by a direct action against the seller of the defective product for breach of the implied terms laid down by the Sale of Goods Act 1979. The most important of those terms are the implied condition that goods are of merchantable quality (s. 14(2)) and the implied condition that the goods are fit for the purpose for which they were obtained (s. 14(3)). Both conditions create strict liability in the sense that the seller is liable for hidden defects.

The use of the Sale of Goods Act 1979 is able in many cases to simulate a direct action by the victim against the negligent manufacturer. The victim can sue the seller for breach of implied term and the seller may in turn commence proceedings under the Sale of Goods Act against the person from whom he obtained supplies; this process is capable of continuing until ultimate liability is returned to the manufacturer of the product. In practice, however, matters are rarely so easy; insolvency, untraceability and the existence of valid exclusion clauses along the chain of distribution may well break the flow of liability.

As far as the person suffering loss from a defective product is concerned, the contractual remedy has two important limitations. The first stems from the fact that an action is available only where there is privity of contract between the supplier and the victim. Thus, if the person suffering loss is the recipient of a gift of the product, a member of the purchaser's family or an independent third party who simply happens to be in the vicinity of the defective product, he cannot bring an action against the supplier of the product. The second deficiency of the contractual solution is that s. 14 of the Sale of Goods Act 1979 imposes liability only upon a seller who has sold the product in the course of a business. Thus, any defective item purchased second-hand from a private individual cannot be the subject of an action under s. 14.

1.2   Pressures for Reform

1.2.1   Early initiatives

Pressure for reform of the common law negligence-based system of compensation for damage caused by defective products began in earnest in the 1970s. By this time the courts of the United States had established the strict liability of manufacturers for defects in their products. This had been achieved not by modifying the rules of tort but by attacking the doctrine of privity of contract and permitting an action against the manufacturer for breach of an implied 'running warranty' of quality. Legislation had also been effected in a variety of common law and civil jurisdictions fixing the manufacturer of a defective product with strict liability for damage caused by the product.

A number of international bodies sought to extend and harmonise the notion of strict liability. The United Nations Commission on International Trade Law had many discussions on this subject, and conventions were produced by the Standing Conference on Private International Law in 1973 (the Hague Convention) and by the Council of Europe in 1977 (the Strasbourg Convention). In the same period the EEC adopted a policy of introducing a Community-wide law imposing strict liability upon the manufacturers of defective products, although it did no more in the 1970s than to produce draft Directives for discussion between member States.

1.2.2 Domestic moves towards reform

International developments resulted directly in the English and Scottish Law Commissions considering the question of strict liability. The Commissions produced a Joint Working Paper in 1975 and a Joint Final Report in 1979, Cmnd 6831. Although the English and Scottish Commissions differed on some points of detail, their conclusion was nevertheless that some system of strict liability should be introduced. The Pearson Commission, which reported in 1978 and which had been appointed in the aftermath of the thalidomide tragedy to consider personal injury compensation, anticipated the findings of the Law Commissions, although again there were minor differences of detail between the Pearson recommendations and those of the Law Commissions.

Despite the broad degree of consensus that some move towards strict liability was necessary, Parliament took no action until the Council of the European Communities issued the final form of its Directive on product liability on 25 July 1985 (Directive 85/374/EEC). Member States were, under art. 19, given three years from that day to introduce into their domestic laws provisions necessary to comply with the Directive. Part I of the Consumer Protection Act 1987 is intended to have this effect in the United Kingdom.

1.3 The Product Liability Directive

1.3.1 Reasons for the Directive

The introduction of a uniform code of product liability within the European Community is perceived by the Community authorities as being necessary to bring about two broad sets of objectives: consumer protection objectives and market unity objectives.

The importance of consumer protection is recognised by the second recital of the product liability Directive, which states that:

> . . . liability without fault on the part of the producer is the sole means of adequately solving the problem, peculiar to our age of increasing technicality, of a fair apportionment of the risks inherent in modern technological production.

This broad statement encompasses a number of distinct arguments in favour of strict liability:

(a)   The general desire to spread loss throughout society rather than to allow it to fall on individual consumers.

(b)   The belief that producers can insure against third-party risks at a lower cost than individual consumers could insure against first-party risks, so that strict liability is the cheapest form of risk-spreading.

(c)   The possibility that strict liability will provide manufacturers with the incentive to increase safety and standards generally, an incentive which is not diminished by the probable existence of liability insurance, given the dangers of premium-rating and of adverse publicity.

(d)   The illogicality and expense of maintaining a fault-based system.

The market unity arguments for strict liability are rather more subtle. The first recital of the Directive asserts that:

. . . the existing divergences [between the laws of member States] may distort competition and affect the movement of goods within the common market and entail a differing degree of protection of the consumer.

Two distinct issues are at stake here:

(a)   The principle that goods must be allowed to move freely between member States, enshrined in arts. 30 to 36 of the Treaty of Rome, is overriden by mandatory consumer protection laws which prevent the sale of dangerous goods, imported or otherwise. By imposing strict liability, standards will improve and goods will be permitted to circulate more freely as between member States.

(b)   If the laws of one member State are less generous to manufacturers than the laws of other member States, by the imposition of strict liability, those manufacturers subject to strict liability will be at a competitive disadvantage when exporting to member States offering a lesser degree of consumer protection. This is so because their products will be more expensive, either as a result of the costs of higher safety standards or as a result of the price of the goods containing an element representing domestic liability insurance premiums. Failure to implement strict liability is thus seen as a form of indirect protectionism.

1.3.2   Structure of the Directive

The product liability Directive consists of 18 preliminary recitals which set out the objectives and broad principles of the Directive, followed by 22 articles which contain the substantive rules. The articles are the legislative element of the Directive, but it is permissible to look to the recitals for general guidance in the event of uncertainty.

The obligation of member States is to legislate in accordance with the general principles of the Directive. National legislation is not permitted to be inconsistent with the Directive, and any member State which fails to comply with the Directive may be taken before the European Court of Justice in accordance with the general provisions of Part Five of the Treaty of Rome. It is not yet settled whether a person in a member State can sue another person under the terms of a Directive which has not been properly implemented by domestic legislation, although the European Court of Justice has expressed the view that this is not possible: *Marshall* v *Southampton and South West Hampshire Area Health Authority (Teaching)* case 152/84 [1986] QB 401. The product liability Directive seeks to avoid conflicts of this sort by providing, in art. 20, that member States are to communicate to the European Commission the texts of their main implementing provisions.

1.3.3   Scope of the Directive

Article 1 of the Directive provides, quite simply, that, 'The producer shall be liable for damage caused by a defect in his product'. Much of the remainder of the article defines the concepts of 'producer', 'damage', 'defect' and 'product'; these matters are discussed in subsequent chapters. It might be noted initially, however, that the Directive is concerned only with liability to 'consumers' (art. 9) and imposes liability only on business suppliers (art. 7(c)).

One interesting feature of the Directive is that it permits three 'derogations', i.e., matters in respect of which each member State is free to determine whether or not it wishes to follow the terms of the Directive. The derogations are as follows:

(a) Agricultural products and game. Article 1 of the Directive provides that there is to be no strict liability upon the producers of these products, although art. 15.1(a) permits member States to impose such liability if they so wish. The UK has chosen not to establish strict liability, in line with what is understood to be the general view of the other member States (see chapter 3).

(b) A 'development risks' defence. The Directive contains, in art. 7(e), a defence open to a manufacturer to the effect that the state of scientific and technical knowledge was not such as to enable the defect to be discovered when the product was put into circulation. However, art. 15.1(b) allows member States to extend strict liability to cover development risks of this nature. It would appear that the majority of member States intend to avail themselves of the derogation, but the UK has again opted to follow the Directive and to retain the defence (see chapter 3).

(c) Maximum liability. Article 16 allows the imposition of a maximum liability in respect of individual claims or in respect of aggregate claims arising out of a particular defect in a product, of some £40 million. The UK did not think it necessary to limit liability in this way (see chapter 4).

The operation of these three derogations is to be assessed in July 1995 to determine whether they should be abandoned or made mandatory.

In addition to these derogations, the Directive is stated to be without prejudice to rights existing under domestic law relating to liability for defective products (art. 13). Moreover, national law is to be referred to in order to determine a number of aspects of product liability. These include the rights *inter se* of persons liable under the Directive (art. 5) and the availability of damages in respect of damage to the defective product itself, economic loss and pain and suffering (art. 9).

1.4 Part I of the Consumer Protection Act 1987

1.4.1 The Directive and the Act
The object of Part I of the Act is to implement the Directive; it has been made abundantly clear by the government that nothing in the s. 1(1) Act is intended to go beyond the protection required by the Directive. In the event of any ambiguity in the Act, the relevant provision is to be construed in accordance with the terms of the Directive. However, s. 1(1) the Directive is not appended to the Act and is not deemed to be a part of the Act.

1.4.2 General features of the Act
By way of introduction to the Act, two of its features should be noted. First, actions under the Act are classified as tortious for the purpose of any enactment conferring jurisdiction upon any court. This is s. 6(7) important in two respects: for determining whether an action is to be commenced in the English High Court or in a county court; and, where one of the parties is domiciled elsewhere in the European Community, for determining whether the English courts or the courts of that other member State have jurisdiction over the dispute. It is

perhaps unfortunate that the Act did not simply classify actions under it as tortious for all purposes: other matters for which classification may have important implications include: the measure of damages, causation, principles of limitation, the recognition and enforcement of judgments given elsewhere in the EEC, the jurisdiction of the English courts *vis-à-vis* courts outside the European Community, and the proper law to be applied to an action in the English courts between nationals of different States.

Interestingly enough, the assumption of Parliament seems to have been that actions under the Act are not tortious for all purposes. On this basis it was thought necessary to amend both the Torts (Interference with Goods) Act 1977, to make it clear that references to proceedings for wrongful interference with goods under that Act include references to proceedings under Part I of the 1987 Act, and s. 16(2) of the Employment Act 1982, to ensure that in the unlikely event of a trade union supplying defective products its liability is unlimited in line with the ordinary tortious rule.

sch. 4,
para. 5
sch. 4,
para. 8

Secondly, the Act, following art. 13 of the Directive, is stated to be without prejudice to other domestic rights in respect of defective products. There will be few cases in which the victim of a defect in a product who is entitled to sue the manufacturer under the Act will be advantaged by proceeding at common law, although it might be noted that the limitation periods under the Act are less generous than those available for negligence actions (see chapter 6). However, many consumers will continue to pursue their rights under the Sale of Goods Act 1979 in order to obtain indemnity for any loss, not the least because damages available under the Sale of Goods Act 1979, unlike the Consumer Protection Act 1987, cover the loss of the defective product itself. Where the Sale of Goods Act 1979 is relied upon, it should be noted that the Consumer Protection Act 1987, like the Directive, is of no assistance to the person sued as it is limited to the protection of 'consumers': a supplier who is sued under the Sale of Goods Act 1979 by a purchaser, has no rights against the original manufacturer under the Consumer Protection Act 1987 but must continue, as before, to proceed against his own supplier under the Sale of Goods Act 1979.

s. 2(6)

sch. 1

s. 5(2)

s. 5(3)

1.4.3 Funding of strict liability

A major objection to the Act during its passage through Parliament was that the insurance necessary to protect producers against claims for strict liability was unobtainable. Suggested solutions to this possible problem were the establishment of a fall-back insurance fund administered by the State or direct payment by the State to the victim where insurance had not been obtainable. However, qualified reassurance on this point was provided by the Association of British Insurers which stated that:

> Insurance companies are by and large confident that they will be able to provide cover for liabilities under the new legislation for current limits of indemnity at premium levels which will have only a marginal effect on the cost of production. There would, however, be a reduction in the amount of insurance capacity if the state of the art defence were not included.

Insurers thus saw no difficulty in coping with potential unlimited liability in respect of any one claim or defect in a product, given the current levels of compensation awarded by the English courts, but in effect demanded the inclusion of the development risks defence. The s. 4(1)(e) attitude of the government to derogations concerning these matters, set out in the Directive, is doubtless at least partially explained by this advice.

Moves to make product liability insurance compulsory were rejected by the government, largely on the basis that reputable manufacturers insure in the ordinary course of events. There will nevertheless be extreme cases, doubtless involving 'unscrupulous' manufacturers, in which consumers will find themselves without an effective remedy due to lack of insurance cover.

Chapter 2

Persons Liable for Defective Products

2.1   Scope of the Act

2.1.1   Persons facing liability

s. 2(1)   The Consumer Protection Act 1987 identifies four classes of person who face liability for the supply of a defective product: the manufacturer; the importer into the EEC; any person who holds himself out as being the manufacturer; and, in the event that none of the above persons can be identified, the person supplying the product in question to the victim. All of the above classes of person are deemed to be 'producers' by art. 3 of the product liability Directive, although the Act has rejected this artificial concept and confines the

s. 1(2)   use of the word 'producer' to the first of the above classes of person. The scheme of the Act is to impose initial liability upon the producer, proclaimed producer or importer. A mere supplier faces liability only where one or more of those facing primary liability cannot be identified. The producer may thus be said to be under primary liability, whereas the mere supplier is under a secondary liability, based upon his inability to identify the producer; this terminology will be adopted throughout the present chapter.

It may be seen that the Act does not create the much criticised system of 'enterprise liability' which operates in some other legal systems and which imposes strict liability upon every person in the manufacturing and distribution chains. The main objection to that system is that it forces every potential defendant to insure against possible liability, thus increasing the cost of the ultimate product to the consumer.

Liability is confined to a person within the above categories who

s. 4(1)(b)   'supplies' the defective product. The word 'supply' is defined broadly

s. 46   and covers all forms of voluntary transfer, whether by way of sale, hire or gift, so that liability will attach whenever a person potentially liable under the Act voluntarily puts a product into circulation. The concept of supply is discussed in more detail in 16.1. A person who

s. 4(1)(b)   has not supplied a product but, for example, has had a product stolen from him which later appears on the market, is granted an express defence to an action in relation to a defect by a victim.

2.1.2   Crown liability

The Act is stated to bind the Crown, but is subject to the usual s. 9(1) limitations on suing the Crown contained in the Crown Proceedings s. 9(2) Act 1947. Supply by, for example, the National Health Service, would thus appear to be within the Act. The prohibition on service personnel suing the Crown as employer in respect of injuries was abolished by the Crown Proceedings (Armed Forces) Act 1987, so that the Crown now faces liability to service personnel in respect of defective products supplied by it.

2.2   Producers

Three classes of person are treated as producers by the Act: s. 1(2) manufacturers, suppliers and processers.   s. 2(2)(a)

2.2.1   Manufacturers

The term 'manufacturer' is not defined in the Act, but in accordance s. 2(2)(a) with art. 3 of the Directive must be taken to refer to 'the manufacturer of a finished product, the producer of any raw material or the manufacturer of a component part'. The situation in which a finished product is defective by virtue of a defect in a raw material or component part supplied by another person gives rise to some difficulty under the Act. The general principle contained in the fourth recital of the Directive is that in these circumstances both the manufacturer of the finished product and the supplier of the defective raw material or component part are liable for the ultimate defect in the finished product. The application of this concept is not, however, free from difficulty.

2.2.1.1   Liability of the manufacturer   As far as the manu-facturer is concerned, the Act provides that: s. 1(3)

> . . . a person who supplies any product in which products are comprised, whether by virtue of being component parts or raw materials or otherwise, shall not be treated by reason only of his supply of that product as supplying any of the products so comprised.

At first sight this wording would appear to indicate that the manufacturer is not to be held liable for a defect in a constituent product unless he has in some way added to the constituent product

or has subjected it to an industrial process in order to incorporate it into the finished product. However, what appears to be intended is to make it clear that a manufacturer is liable for a defect in the finished product only by virtue of the fact that he has supplied the finished product. Consequently, where he is for some reason not liable for defects in the finished product itself, for example, if the product is excluded from the Act, he cannot be liable for defects in the constituent parts of that finished product. There is, however, an exception in respect of buildings: the builder of a defective building
s. 46(3)(4) (or his employer) is not liable for the supply of the building, but the Act deems him to be the supplier of any of the components used to make up the building.

In the result, then, the manufacturer of a product is liable for any
s. 1(3)   defects in the product, whether or not caused by defective constituent parts. His liability is, however, based conceptually on his supply of the finished product and not on his supply of the elements which go to make up that finished product.

2.2.1.2   Liability of the supplier of the raw material or constituent part   The supplier of a raw material or constituent part would appear not to be liable for damage caused by a defect in the finished product where his own contributory element of the finished product was not of itself defective. This is not explicit from the Act itself but it is stated in the fourth recital to the Directive that a person is liable only in respect of defective products which he himself has supplied, and the supplier of a raw material or component part cannot be said to have supplied the finished product. However, such a person is
s. 1(2)   liable, as a manufacturer under the Act in his own right for any defect in his subsidiary product which makes the finished product defective; his liability does not cease once his product has been incorporated into the finished product.

One unanswered question here is whether the supplier of a defective component is liable for damage to the finished product caused by that component; an example might be damage to a car, assembled and supplied by manufacturer A, due to a fault in its
s. 5(2)   battery, supplied by manufacturer B. The Act specifically provides that a producer is not to be liable for any loss or damage caused by the defective component to the finished product in which it is incorporated, so that in the example above neither manufacturer A nor manufacturer B would face liability for damage caused by the battery to the car. Manufacturer B's liability under the Act is limited to those cases in which the finished car causes damage to some other property or results in personal injury.

However, the Directive is worded rather differently. Article 9(b) simply provides that there is to be no liability for 'damage to, or destruction of, . . . the defective product itself'. This wording would appear to exempt manufacturer A, as the product supplied by him— the car—is the only product which has suffered damage. However, the Directive would appear to impose liability upon manufacturer B, on the basis that art. 9(b) provides him with a defence only in respect of damage to his own product, the battery. The car as the finished product in which the battery was incorporated is clearly not 'the defective product itself' referred to in art. 9(b) as the car was not supplied by manufacturer B. If this reasoning is correct, there is a conflict between Act and Directive concerning the liability of manufacturer B.

Where the supplier of a defective raw material or constituent part does face liability, i.e., where the item supplied by him causes personal injury or damage to property other than to the finished product itself, the Act provides a specific defence. He can escape s. 4(1)(f) liability to the victim if he can show that the defect in the item supplied by him can also be regarded as a defect in the finished product and was wholly attributable to the design of the finished product or to his compliance with instructions given by the manufacturer of the finished product.

2.2.2 Suppliers of raw materials   s. 1(2)
Liability attaches to a person who has won or abstracted a substance which has not been manufactured.

2.2.3 Processors of natural products   s. 1(2)
Liability is imposed in respect of a product which has not been manufactured, won or abstracted but the essential characteristics of which are attributable to an industrial or other process having been carried out. The purpose of this provision is to catch a person who processes a natural product, for example, an agricultural product, for resale; agricultural products themselves are excluded from the Act. The drafting is not, however, entirely happy, for the Act requires that the essential characteristics of the product must stem from the processing: is the essential characteristic of a tin of peas the peas themselves or the fact that they have been tinned? Article 2 of the Directive is simpler, and seemingly wider, in providing that the processor becomes liable for a defect arising from any initial processing.

2.3 'Own-branders'

s. 2(1)(b)   The term 'own-brander' is not one used by the Act, but it is a useful denotation of the person described by the Act as one who, by putting his name on the product or using a trade mark or other distinguishing mark (as defined by the Trade Marks Act 1938, s. 68), has held himself out to be the producer of the product. The essence of the liability of an own-brander in respect of a product is that he has, in the words of art. 3 of the Directive, presented himself as its producer. This would undoubtedly apply to the case of a retailer who sells own-brand goods manufactured by another, and to the case of an importer who attaches his own imprint to goods. The Act is not, however, intended to extend to a retail pharmacist who affixes his own label to a drug provided on prescription; it is thought that the pharmacist does not hold himself out as being the manufacturer of the drug by so doing. Nevertheless, it may be the case that a pharmacist who amalgamates two or more drugs is a 'producer' of the resultant concoction and is thus liable for a defect in any of the constituent drugs; in such a case, it is thought that the pharmacist would be able to recover a full indemnity from the manufacturer of the defective drug under the Civil Liability (Contribution) Act 1978 (see 2.6).

The Act arguably appears not to cover the common situation in which a licensing agreement between manufacturers allows manufacturer B to produce goods bearing manufacturer A's trade mark or name. B himself is clearly liable as the producer, albeit unnamed, but it would appear that A may escape liability even though his name appears on the product. This is so because A has neither 'put his name' on the product nor has he 'used a trade mark or other distinguishing mark', as both of these acts have been performed by B; at best, A has facilitated these acts, but this is seemingly not sufficient for the purposes of the Act.

s. 2(3)   The general scheme of the Act in respect of a retailer is to render him liable only where the producer of the product is unidentifiable but to provide the retailer with a defence where he, at the victim's request, identifies the person who supplied him with the goods; see 2.5. In the case of an own-brander, however, liability cannot be

s. 2(2)(b)   evaded by identifying the manufacturer or supplier to him; the liability of an own-brander is a primary liability, and is not the secondary liability facing retailers.

2.4   Importers

s. 2(2)(c)   The liability of an importer under the Act requires three elements to be satisfied: importation into the EEC, supply to another, and doing these things in the course of a business.

2.4.1 Importation into the EEC

The product must have been imported into a member State of the s. 2(2)(c)
EEC from a place outside the EEC. Thus, if a television
manufactured in Japan is imported into the United Kingdom, the
importer is liable as being the first importer of the product into the
EEC. However, if a television manufactured in Germany is imported
into the United Kingdom, the importer faces no liability, as there was
no import from a place outside the EEC.

The position of reimporters is open to doubt. Thus, if a television
manufactured in Germany is exported to the United States, and is
then imported into the United Kingdom, the importer at first sight
appears to be liable for defects. It is far from certain that this is the
correct view, given that the object of imposing liability upon
importers into the EEC is the possible difficulty of an action being
mounted outside the EEC against the original manufacturer; in the
case in question, however, the original manufacturer is present within
the EEC and can be sued as the producer of a defective product.

2.4.2 Course of business

The importer must have obtained the product in order, in the course s. 2(2)(c)
of any business, to supply it to another. The term 'business' is defined s. 45(1)
as including a trade or profession and the activities of a professional
or trade association or of a local authority or other public authority.
The importer's liability rests upon his intention at the date of the
importation; a motor dealer in the United Kingdom who imports a
Japanese car for his own use is not liable for defects in it which
become manifest after he has resold the car either privately or even in
the course of his business (if it had not been his intention to resell in
the course of his business at the date of importation).

2.4.3 Supply

The importer must supply the product. As noted above, the word s. 2(2)(c)
'supply' extends to all forms of voluntary transfer. In practice, the s. 46
importer will be the supplier to other dealers rather than to the public.

2.5 Suppliers

The supplier of a defective product does not face primary liability s. 2(3)
under the Act where he is not the producer, nor an own-brander, nor
the importer into the EEC, although he will face liability towards any
purchaser from him under the Sale of Goods Act 1979 if the product
is not of merchantable quality or not fit for its purpose. The Directive
nevertheless imposes what may be regarded as a secondary liability
upon every supplier, whether he is the retailer or an intermediate

supplier, if the persons under primary liability cannot be identified. Such liability is stated by the fourth recital to the Directive as being necessary for the protection of consumers. As explained below, the Act would seem to be somewhat wider in its impact than art. 3 of the Directive. The elements of supplier liability are as follows.

2.5.1   Request by victim

s. 2(3)(a)   The person suffering the damage must request the supplier to identify one or more of the persons facing primary liability under the Act. For all practical purposes the request will normally be limited to identification of one or both of the producer of the finished product and of the importer into the EEC, as other persons who face primary liability under the Act are excluded either as a matter of practicality

s. 2(2)(b)   or as a matter of law. Thus the affixer of a trade mark or other identifying mark to the finished product necessarily identifies himself. Moreover, if the name of the producer is required by the victim, the obligation on the supplier is to identify only the producer of the finished product and not any producers or abstractors of

s. 1(3)   component parts and raw materials: the Act provides, for this purpose, that the supplier of a finished product is not to be taken, by reason of that supply, also to supply the component parts and raw materials which go to make up the product.

s. 2(3)(a)   It would seem from the wording of the Act that the supplier may be requested to make an identification even where the victim is aware of the identities of one of the persons who face primary liability under the Act and where that person is solvent. In other words, the victim may demand to know the identities of every person potentially facing a primary liability, other than those responsible for producing component parts and raw materials.

2.5.2   Request within a reasonable time

s. 2(3)(b)   The request must be made within a reasonable period after the damage occurs. What is reasonable is a matter of fact in every case. The Act is rather vague about when damage occurs, for there are a number of possibilities, including:

    (a)   the date at which damage began to occur;
    (b)   the date at which the damage became significant;
    (c)   the date at which the victim ought to have become aware that damage had occurred (discoverability);
    (d)   the date at which the victim did become aware that damage had occurred.

    The Act does provide a definition of the date at which damage to

s. 5(5)–(7) property occurs, which is the 'discoverability' date set out in (c) above, but while that definition is stated to be applicable to all of Part I of the Act it appears in the limited context of ascertaining whether a product was, at the date of damage, intended for consumer or commercial use (see chapter 4). Moreover, that definition makes no mention of the date of damage for personal injury claims, which is hardly surprising given the context in which it appears. These factors suggest that the date of the occurrence of damage is, for present purposes, undefined. It is nevertheless suggested that the discoverability test ought to be adopted for the purposes of notifying requests to suppliers; this would serve to maintain consistency in Part I of the Act, and would also bring the Act into line with the Limitation Act 1980 and the Latent Damage Act 1986, both of which adopt discoverability tests for cases in which personal injury and damage to property may not be readily discoverable. `s. 5(3)` `s. 5(5)–(7)` `sch. 1`

If this is the proper test, damage may be taken to have occurred at the earliest time at which the victim knew or ought to have known, from facts ascertainable by him alone or with the help of expert advice which ought reasonably to have been taken, that damage had occurred. The damage must, however, have been sufficiently serious to lead a reasonable person to initiate proceedings in respect of it. This definition is considered in more detail in chapter 6. `s. 5(5)` `s. 5(7)` `s. 5(6)`

2.5.3 Impracticability of identification by victim

The request to the supplier for identification of persons primarily liable must be made at a time at which it is not reasonably practicable for the victim himself to identify all of those persons. This wording again confirms that if the victim could reasonably identify some, but not all, of the persons primarily liable, a request may be made to the supplier. `s. 2(3)(b)` `s. 2(3)(a)`

2.5.4 Failure of supplier to comply with request

The supplier's secondary liability arises if, following a request by the victim, he fails to disclose one of two types of information: the identifications requested or the identity of the person who supplied the product to him. Where either of these pieces of information is given to the victim, the supplier ceases to be liable under the Act. This is important, for it demonstrates that the supplier's role is merely to identify the potential defendants; if he does so, and it proves to be the case that all of those defendants are insolvent or outside the jurisdiction of the English courts, the supplier remains free from liability. Supplier liability is not, therefore, a fall-back for the victim, but is based on the notion that commercial suppliers who themselves deal with unidentified suppliers must bear any risk of defects in their products. `s. 2(3)(c)`

s. 2(3)(c)   The first class of information that relieves the supplier from liability is the identities of those persons facing primary liability and requested by the victim. The supplier does not fulfil this duty by identifying one person who may be sued by the victim. Thus if the victim asks the supplier to identify the producer of the product, the supplier does not escape liability by identifying the importer, even if the importer is solvent and within the jurisdiction.

s. 2(3)(c)   The second class of information that relieves the supplier from liability is the identity of the person from whom he obtained the product. It is possible, and indeed probable, however, that the person identified by the supplier will not be the manufacturer or importer and will thus not face primary liability under the Act. What is contemplated by the Act in these circumstances is that the victim must make the same request, for identification of one or more persons primarily liable to him, to the person identified to him by the supplier, and that this process continues until the victim finally obtains from someone the information actually required by him. The problem posed by this process is the requirement of the Act that the

s. 2(3)(c)   request is made within a reasonable time of damage occurring; if the chain of supply is a long one, reasonable time for the making of requests may possibly expire without any useful information having been obtained from persons secondarily liable concerning persons primarily liable.

2.5.5   Supply in the course of a business

s. 2(2)(c)   The supplier must have supplied the product in the course of a
s. 45(1)   business. Thus if the victim is injured by a product purchased second-hand from a private individual or from any person not selling in the course of a business, that person does not face secondary liability under the Act and is not obliged to reveal the identity of the supplier to him or the producer of the product in question.

2.5.6   Death of the victim

There may be extreme cases in which the defect in the product has caused fatal injury to the consumer. Under the general law damages for fatal injuries can be recovered by the victim's personal representatives for his estate under the Law Reform (Miscellaneous Provisions) Act 1934 and by certain of his relatives under the Fatal

s. 6(2)   Accidents Act 1976. The Consumer Protection Act 1987 provides, in effect, that the request for identification may be made by the victim's personal representatives under the 1934 Act and his relatives under the 1976 Act, and that the supplier is liable to them in damages assessable under those Acts if he fails to comply with their requests for identification.

2.6   Concurrent Liability

It will frequently be the case that more than one person is liable to the victim under the Act for damage arising from a defect. Where this occurs, their liability is to be joint and several. The consequence, as s. 2(5) far as the victim is concerned, is that each person liable may be sued for the full amount of the victim's loss.

The Act leaves open the question of the rights of persons jointly and severally liable as between themselves, but art. 5 of the Directive stipulates that this matter is to be determined by domestic law. In England the matter is governed by the Civil Liability (Contribution) Act 1978. This Act provides that any person liable in respect of damage may recover contribution from any other person liable in respect of the same damage. There is no fixed formula for determining the amount recoverable, and the question is to be determined by the court in accordance with what is just and equitable having regard to the extent of responsibility for the damage. The amount of contribution may, therefore, range between nothing and full indemnity. It ought to be possible, therefore, for the ultimate liability for damage arising from a defect to be passed on to the person responsible, which will normally be the manufacturer of the defective product. The exercise of contribution rights as between persons liable, and the ultimate incidence of liability is not, however, of concern to the victim, who may sue whichever of the potential defendants he chooses.

Contribution proceedings in respect of liability under the Act are governed by s. 10 of the Limitation Act 1980, which provides that the plaintiff in such proceedings has two years from the date of judgment or award against him, or from the date of any settlement, to issue a writ. However, unless the proceedings are commenced within 10 sch. 1 years from the date at which the defective product was first put into circulation, they become time-barred. The latter position is consistent with that of the victim himself (see chapter 5) and arises as a result of the fact that the Consumer Protection Act 1987 operates to extinguish claims not brought within the 10-year period; time-limits sch. 1, which extinguish claims operate also to extinguish the right to sue for para. 1 contribution even though the two-year time-limit laid down by the Limitation Act 1980 for bringing contribution proceedings has not expired (Civil Liability (Contribution) Act 1978, s. 1(3)).

2.7   Defences

As noted above, liability attaches under the Act only where the product has been supplied by the producer and in the course of his

business. To make this clear, it is provided specifically in the
s. 4   defences section of the Act that the person proceeded against is not to
s. 4(1)(b)   be liable if he can show that he did not at any time supply the product
s. 4(1)(c)   or if the only supply of the product by him was otherwise than in the
course of his business.

Chapter 3

Products within the Act

3.1 General Definition of 'Product'

A 'product' is defined for the purposes of Part I of the Consumer Protection Act 1987 as any goods or electricity, and any product comprised in another product whether as a component part or as raw material. The word 'goods' is itself defined as including substances, growing crops and things comprised in land by being attached to it, ships, aircraft and vehicles. Some of these terms are also given a definition: 'substance' means any natural or artificial solid, vaporous or liquid substance; 'ship' includes any boat or other vessel used in navigation; 'aircraft' includes any glider, balloon or hovercraft; and 'vehicle' (which is undefined but is presumably wider than the defined term 'motor vehicle') includes any mechanically propelled vehicle intended or adapted for use on the roads (Road Traffic Act 1972, s. 190(1)).

s. 1(2)
s. 45(1)

s. 45(1)

s. 45(1)
s. 45(1)

s. 45(1)

It would seem to follow from these definitions that almost anything, whether movable or immovable, manufactured, processed or developed, will be a 'product'. However, art. 2 of the product liability Directive defines the term 'product' more restrictively by omitting immovables and primary agricultural products. Moreover, art. 14 goes on to exclude loss or damage caused by nuclear accidents and covered by international conventions, so that products manufactured by or making use of nuclear power are to that extent outside the Directive. It has consequently been necessary to make provision in the Consumer Protection Act 1987 for the exclusion of these three forms of product.

3.2 Immovables (Buildings)

3.2.1 Supply of buildings

Buildings are deemed not to be products under art. 2 of the Directive. The exclusion of buildings from the Consumer Protection Act 1987 operates in rather a different way. A building would appear to fall within the general definition of 'goods', and thus prima facie to be

s. 45(1)

within the Act, but the Act provides that goods comprised in land are
s. 46(4)   deemed not to be supplied where the supply is effected by the creation
or disposal of an interest in land. Consequently, the supply of a
building by its builder under a contract of sale or by virtue of a lease is
outside the product liability provisions of the Act, so that if the
building is defective and causes personal injury or damage to other
property, no liability attaches to the builder.

The exclusion of buildings is to some extent compensated for in
England by the Defective Premises Act 1972, which establishes
strict liability for defects in dwelling-houses. However, as a matter of
practice, given the short limitation period set out in the 1982 Act and
the propensity of defects in buildings not to become manifest
immediately, actions in respect of defective and dangerous buildings
tend to be brought at common law under general negligence
principles.

3.2.2   Supply of constituent parts of buildings

s. 46(4)   Although the supply of a building does not attract liability in respect
of defects in the building itself, the person constructing a building is
s. 46(3)   nevertheless deemed to be the supplier of the individual products
which constitute that building. Thus, as noted above, if a building
collapses and causes personal injury or damage because it has been
improperly designed, the Act will not apply. However, if a building
collapses due to a defect in one of its constituent parts, such as the
cement used for the foundations, and causes personal injury or
damage to property, liability will attach to the builder as the supplier
of the cement. It might be added that the supplier of the defective
product to the builder will himself face liability to the ultimate victim.

In ascertaining the scope of liability for a defective constituent
part, it is important to bear in mind the principle contained in the Act
which, contrary to the terms of art. 9(b) of the Directive (see 2.2.1.2)
s. 5(2)   provides that the supplier of a defective constituent product is not to
be liable for damage caused by it to the finished product. In other
words, the supplier of any defective part in a building, whether he is
the manufacturer of that product or the builder himself, faces liability
under the Act only where the defect results in personal injury or
damage to property other than the building itself.

3.3   Agricultural Products

3.3.1   General definition

The third recital of the Directive states that 'it is appropriate to
exclude liability for agricultural products and game', and art. 2
provides that the Directive does not apply to 'primary agricultural

products'. This term is defined by art. 2 as meaning 'the products of the soil, of stock-farming and of fisheries'. The Act follows this wording closely, defining agricultural produce as 'any produce of the soil, of stock-farming or of fisheries'. Game is not mentioned by the Act.   s. 1(2)

The term 'products of the soil' raises interesting questions for the modern technique of hydroponics, which enables crops to be grown in vitamin-enriched sand or water. It may well be that the phrase will have to be interpreted as referring to products which are capable of being grown in the soil, in order to extend the exemption to hydroponically grown matter.   s. 1(2)

3.3.2 Justification of the exclusion

The reason for the exclusion of agricultural products does not appear in the Directive, although the fact that the decision was far from obvious is made clear by art. 15.1(a), which allows any member State to provide, by way of derogation, that agricultural products and game are to fall within their strict liability laws. It is not at this stage clear how many of the member States will avail themselves of this relaxation, and there is some expectation that the exclusion will be removed on the review of the Directive in 1995.

There are strong reasons for including agricultural produce within any regime of product liability. First, food poisoning is, as far as the consumer is concerned, in essence no different in nature from any other form of personal injury inflicted by a defective product. Secondly, in the English context the exclusion would appear to be anomalous. The seller of a harmful foodstuff may be sued by the purchaser under the Sale of Goods Act 1979, and the chain of liability will frequently be followed back to the original supplier by a series of actions under that Act; consequently, it cannot be argued that producer liability would be an innovation. The weakness of the contractual remedy is that it does not permit an action by any person not in privity with the seller, such as a member of the purchaser's family; the exclusion of foodstuffs from the Consumer Protection Act 1987 merely serves to reinforce this curious position and may pave the way for judicial ingenuity in fashioning remedies (see *Lockett* v *A. & M. Charles Ltd* [1938] 4 All ER 170, which probably cannot survive the general approach of the House of Lords in *Woodar Investment Development Ltd* v *Wimpey Construction UK Ltd* [1980] 1 All ER 571). The Pearson Commission had been vigorously in favour of including agricultural produce within its scheme for product liability.

Whatever the merits of these points, the decision not to take advantage of the permitted derogation in the Directive was based on a series of other considerations:

(a)   Any decision by the UK to impose liability upon farmers and other producers might put them at a competitive disadvantage within the EEC if other countries chose to maintain the exemption.

(b)   There are presently in existence strict rules governing the production and sale of food, under the Food and Environment Protection Act 1985. Contravention of these rules does not, however, give rise to civil liability.

(c)   Small farmers, who are often unable to insure, would find themselves facing claims. It might be noted, however, that the chain of liability which may be established under the Sale of Goods Act 1979 has this effect independently of product liability actions.

(d)   Any liability for agricultural produce would tend to be absolute rather than strict, as establishing ordinary defences would be difficult. In particular, the propensity of food to perish, and the difficulty of fixing the date at which this occurred, might lead to the imposition of liability on farmers for products which had not been defective when supplied by them but which had become defective in the course of their distribution to consumers.

(e)   The imposition of liability might in any event be illusory, as the original suppliers of food products may be difficult to trace, particularly given the practice of 'bulking' the output of small suppliers.

3.3.3   Effect of processing

3.3.3.1 Nature of the liability of processors of agricultural produce   The Directive contains an important exception to the exclusion of primary agricultural products. The third recital provides for liability for agricultural products and game 'where they have undergone a processing of an industrial nature which could cause a defect'. The wording of the implementing article in the Directive is, unfortunately, different in a crucial respect: art. 2 imposes liability in respect of agricultural products 'which have undergone initial processing'.

It is readily apparent that there are significant differences between 'initial' processing and 'industrial' processing, for the latter term implies some alteration in the qualities of the product. Examples of industrial processes might, therefore, be the canning of vegetables and the production of fish fingers. By contrast, there are various activities which might properly be described as 'initial' processes but which do not readily lend themselves to the description 'industrial'. Some illustrations might be: mechanical harvesting, the spraying of crops with fertilisers and pesticides, milk pasteurisation, the use of hormones or antibiotics on animals to be slaughtered for meat, and freezing with the use of additional water or preservatives. It is far from clear whether these more limited activities were intended to attract liability under the Directive, although the matter might be resolved by the general principle of construction that the articles of a Directive are of significantly greater weight than its preliminaries. On this basis, there would have been powerful justification for adopting the words 'initial processing' in any implementing legislation.

The Consumer Protection Act 1987 has nevertheless followed the approach of the recitals rather than that of the Directive itself. This is achieved in two different but to some extent parallel ways. First, the definition of 'producer' under the Act, in relation to a product which has been neither manufactured nor abstracted, is confined to a person who has carried out an 'industrial process' the effect of which is to s. 1(2) establish the 'essential characteristics' of the product. Secondly, liability is removed from all persons against whom actions may potentially be brought under the Act—producers, own-branders, importers into the EEC and mere suppliers (see chapter 2)—in respect of 'any defect in any game or agricultural produce if the only supply of the game or produce by that person to another was at a time when s. 2(4) it had not undergone an industrial process'.

The impact of these provisions is as follows. There can be no liability whatsoever for agricultural products unless they have undergone industrial processing. Further the producer who applies the industrial process can only be liable if the essential characteristics of the resulting product were attributable to that process. This additional requirement does not, however, affect the liability of own-branders, EEC importers and mere suppliers.

Two problems are inherent in this formulation. First, the basic notion that there is to be liability for 'industrial', as opposed to 'initial', processing is incompatible with the clear wording of art. 2 of the Directive. Secondly, the additional 'essential characteristics' test which governs the liability of processors is unauthorised by the Directive and, equally seriously, is bound to give rise to difficulties. By way of example: has fish ceased to have the essential characteristics of fish because it has been incorporated into a fish finger; or are peas no longer essentially peas because they have been canned or frozen? The wording of the Act strongly implies that there is a difference between industrial processing, and industrial processing which affects the essential characteristics of a product, and it is likely that the scope of these concepts will have to be resolved by litigation.

3.3.3.2   The extent of liability for processed agricultural produce   It follows from the wording of the Act that a processor of primary

s. 2(4)   agricultural produce is to be strictly liable not just for defects
introduced at the processing stage, but also for defects which existed
in the produce when it was supplied to him for processing. An
example is as follows. Farmer A supplies a quantity of carrots to
processor B for canning. However, as a result of the use of an
inappropriate pesticide by farmer A, the carrots were poisonous
when supplied to processor B. In these circumstances farmer A is not
liable under the Act (unless, of course, applying a pesticide is an
industrial process which changes the essential character of carrots)
but processor B is liable even though the defect in the carrots was not
attributable to him. The rationale of this is to ensure that commercial
processors of food operate rigid quality control procedures. It might
be added that farmer A in the above example is likely to be the subject
of an action by processor B under the Sale of Goods Act 1979, unless
there is a valid exclusion clause in the contract between them.

One aspect of the Directive raises interesting, although possibly
only theoretical, difficulties in the type of case outlined above. The
third recital states that there is to be liability for primary agricultural
products only where they have undergone 'processing of an industrial
nature *which could cause a defect in these products'* (emphasis added).
This terminology is not used in the main body of the Directive nor in
the Consumer Protection Act 1987, but it seems to leave open the
possibility that the application of a completely safe industrial process
to food exempts the processor from strict liability. It may be that no
industrial process is completely safe, so that the point is not of
significance, but it is curious that the Directive should contemplate
complex evidential analysis of the safety of particular industrial
processes before strict liability can be imposed.

3.4   Products and Nuclear Power

The dangers from the use of nuclear power had been recognised
before the Directive was finalised in 1985, and the pre-existing rules
operating in each of the member States of the EEC conferring
compensation on those harmed by nuclear activities, many of which
owed their existence to international convention, were thought to be
adequate. Consequently injury or damage arising from nuclear
accident is excluded from the Directive by art. 14. The Consumer
Protection Act 1987 implements this principle by stating that nothing
in it is to prejudice the operation of the Nuclear Installations Act
s. 6(8)   1965. However, nothing in the 1965 Act itself provides that liability
for nuclear accidents is to be governed exclusively by its terms, so that
in theory at least it might be possible to mount an action under the
1987 Act where, for example, a product has become contaminated.

The most important features of the Nuclear Installations Act 1965 are as follows:

(a)   The United Kingdom Atomic Energy Authority (UKAEA) alone is entitled to use sites for the installation and operation of nuclear reactors, although other persons may be licensed by the Secretary of State for Energy to do so under nuclear site licences (s. 1).

(b)   The holders of licences, the UKAEA and the British and foreign governments owe a duty to ensure that no injury occurs to persons or to property from the use or transport of nuclear materials or from the emission of radiation (ss. 7-10).

(c)   Breach of duty results in strict liability, although this is subject to a maximum sum for liability and also to a 10-year limitation period (ss. 12 and 16).

Chapter 4

Defects

4.1 Framework and Burden of Proof

Strict liability attaches under the Consumer Protection Act 1987 for products which are 'defective', a term which is carefully defined. There are, however, three classes of defect which do not attract liability: a defect attributable to compliance with any statutory or Community obligation; a defect not present in the product when it was supplied by the defendant; and a defect not discoverable when the defendant put the product into circulation, given the state of scientific knowledge at that date. The definition of 'defect' and these defences will be discussed in this chapter.

s. 3
s. 4(1)(a)
s. 4(1)(d)
s. 4(1)(e)

It should also be noted that the supplier of a defective component part, which is incorporated into a finished product and which causes a defect in the finished product itself, is given a specific defence under the Act. He is entitled to escape liability if he can show either that the defect in the finished product was wholly attributable to its design, or that the component part was designed in accordance with the instructions of the producer of the finished product. The significance of this defence was discussed in chapter 2.

s. 4(1)(f)

The burden of proof under the product liability Directive is clearly stated: the consumer must demonstrate that the product was defective (art. 4) and it is thereafter incumbent on the producer to substantiate any of the above defences (art. 7). The Act does not specify that the consumer must prove the existence of a defect, although this follows from general principle. It is expressly stated that the producer bears the burden of making out a defence.

s. 4(1)

4.2 Meaning of 'Defect'

4.2.1 General definition
In common parlance a product is described as defective when it fails fully or in part to operate in accordance with the common expectations of its manufacturer and purchaser. However, the Act ascribes a far narrower meaning to the word. The Act, following the

wording of art. 6 of the Directive, provides that a product, including its component parts, is defective for the purposes of strict liability only where it is unsafe, i.e., that it poses a danger to persons and to their other property. Consequently, deficiencies in a product which   s. 3(1) defeat reasonable expectations, in that they render the product unfit for its purpose or of unmerchantable quality, but which do not go so far as to make the product dangerous, are outside the Act. The consumer's main—and possibly only—remedy in respect of goods which are safe but useless, is against the person from whom they were obtained, under s. 14 of the Sale of Goods Act 1979.

    The key concept is, therefore, that of 'safety'. A product is defective   s. 3(1) for the purposes of the Act if its safety is not such as persons generally are entitled to expect. The Act does not seek to provide an exhaustive definition of what constitutes a legitimate expectation of safety, and requires the court to take into account all of the surrounding circumstances. Nevertheless, it does provide a list of factors which   s. 3(2) must be taken into account by the court; the weight to be put upon them remains a matter for the court. In broad terms, the Act is concerned with manufacturing defects, design defects, component defects and failure to issue warnings about use.

4.2.2   Statutory elements of a 'defect'

4.2.2.1 Marketing   The court must take into account 'the manner in which, and purposes for which, the product has been marketed, its get-up, the use of any mark in relation to the product and any instructions for, or warnings with respect to, doing or refraining from   s. 3(2)(a) doing anything with or in relation to the product'. This elaborate phraseology implements the comparatively modest requirement of art. 6.1(a) of the Directive that the 'presentation' of the product is to be taken into account.

    The crucial aspect of this provision of the Act is the use of the word 'marketed', which should be distinguished from 'supplied'. The formulation adopted was perceived as going beyond the mechanical process of selling, and extending to the following matters: the reasons for the manufacture of the product; the manner in which the product has been promoted (including, in particular, whether safety or other claims have been made in respect of it); the form in which the product is delivered, both to the dealer and to the ultimate consumer; the adequacy of operating or assembling instructions; warnings about the possible misuse of the product; and the provision of post-sales services including, where appropriate, dealer and customer training.

    It has been suggested that the width of the concept of 'marketing' operates to impose automatic strict liability on the producer of a product which is inherently dangerous. This is not in fact the case, as the Act requires a product to be defective before liability can attach. What is true, however, is that the producer of an inherently dangerous product runs the risk of being held liable unless he conveys clear instructions and warnings about its dangers. For this reason, the producers of razor-blades, of drugs with known side-effects and of matter with combustible qualities are, assuming the presence of adequate warnings, in no greater conceptual danger of a strict liability action than the producer of cotton-wool; a plaintiff consumer who disregards an adequate warning will fail on the basis of his inability to prove that the product was defective. Nevertheless, it is possible to contemplate a certain amount of litigation about the adequacy of warnings: it may, for example, be open to question whether government health warnings on tobacco products are sufficient to exempt their manufacturers from strict liability, subject, of course, to the plaintiff being able to establish to the satisfaction of a court that personal injury suffered by him was caused by tobacco products.

4.2.2.2   Expectations about use   The court must take into account 'what might reasonably be expected to be done with or in relation to the product'. It is not clear from this wording whether the reasonable expectation in question is that of the supplier of the product or of its ultimate user; art. 6.2(b) of the Directive is equally ambiguous. The draftsman of the Act appears to have intended the former interpretation, although the government view is that the distinction is unlikely to be of practical importance. This remains to be seen.

s. 3(2)(b)

It is noteworthy that the concept adopted in both Directive and Act is that of reasonable expectation, as opposed to the more familiar—to English lawyers at least—test of reasonable foreseeability. It is thought that the statutory formulation of expectation is rather wider in scope than foreseeability, as the latter has acquired a limited technical legal meaning.

4.2.2.3   Time of supply   The court must take into account 'the time when the product was supplied by its producer'. What seems to be intended here is the protection of a producer who, at the time when his product was put into circulation, had adhered to the accepted safety standards then prevailing. Thus, the producer of a car without seat-belts cannot be regarded as having supplied a defective product if, at the time of the supply, installing seat-belts had not been compulsory. The Act indeed goes on to state specifically that the fact that a safer product has been supplied at a later date is not without more to be taken into account in assessing the safety of the original product at the date of its supply.

s. 3(2)(c)

s. 3(2)

4.2.2.4 Economic factors? Neither the Directive nor the Act
mentions the costs of making a product safe or the price of the
product. It thus remains open to a producer to argue that the low
price of his product must be taken into account in assessing
reasonable expectations of its level of safety. If this is correct, a cheap
and dangerous product may not be classified as unsafe, even in the
absence of warnings, as persons generally would not be entitled to
expect a product of that price to be safe. Interestingly enough, the
cost of making a product safe is to be taken into account in
determining safety for the purposes of the criminal law, under Part II
of the Act.   s. 10(2)(c)

4.3 Compliance with Statutory or Community Obligations

The person proceeded against under the Act has a defence if he can
show that the defect in the product is attributable to compliance with
any requirement imposed by or under any statutory provision or with s. 4(1)(a)
any Community obligation. The term 'Community obligation' is not
defined in the Consumer Protection Act 1987 itself, although a
general definition is contained in sch. 1 to the European
Communities Act 1972 and this definition is applied to all legislation
by the Interpretation Act 1978, sch. 1.   •

The defence is available only in respect of statutory 'requirements'.
Thus, adherence to a voluntary code, even if authorised by an Act of
Parliament, is not sufficient. An important illustration of the limits of
the defence is to be found in the context of drugs; the supply of a
defective drug will attract strict liability even if that drug has been
awarded an official safety certificate from the Committee on the
Safety of Medicines.

4.4 Defects Arising after Supply

A supplier has a defence under the Act if he can show that the defect
did not exist in the product at the relevant time. The 'relevant time'
varies according to the identity of the defendant. If the person s. 4(1)(d)
proceeded against is a manufacturer, own-brander or importer into
the EEC, the relevant time is the date at which that person supplied
the product to another; in most cases, the purchaser will be a dealer as s. 4(2)(a)
opposed to the ultimate consumer, and it is important to note that the
time at which the product is supplied to the ultimate consumer is not
in itself of significance. If the person proceeded against is a mere
supplier, outside any of the above categories, the relevant time is the
time at which the product was last supplied by a producer,
own-brander or importer into the EEC. The effect of the definition of s. 4(2)(b)

relevant time is perhaps best summarised by the phrase used in art. 7 of the Directive; liability is to be assessed on the date at which the product was put into circulation.

This defence is primarily for the benefit of the manufacturer of a product which is safe when put into circulation but which subsequently develops a defect which is beyond the manufacturer's control. The defect may develop from a number of causes: ordinary wear and tear; inadequate servicing of a technical product by an independent person; or excessive delay by a distributor in selling a perishable product. In addition, technical or other developments taking place since the date at which the product was put into circulation may, with the benefit of hindsight, demonstrate its unsafety. It is far from certain, however, that the defence will be easy to substantiate, for the defendant bears the burden of proving that the

s. 4(1)   product was not defective when put into circulation by him; the line between a product which is defective and a product which bears the scars of ordinary wear and tear may indeed be fine. It might be added that one justification of the exemption of primary agricultural

s. 2(4)   products from the ambit of the Act (see 3.3) was that the difficulty in ascertaining the precise point at which a defect develops in food would have rendered this particular defence largely illusory in that context.

The defence is applicable to defects which have developed subsequently and not to defects of which the defendant became aware subsequently. Thus it is not a defence for a person liable under the Act to provide that he attempted to recall a product which developed a defect before it was put into circulation but of which he had not been aware at that date. At common law, it would appear that a manufacturer may be held to be negligent for failing to recall products within a class which have proved to contain a defect rendering them dangerous (*Walton* v *British Leyland*, 1978).

4.5   Development Risks

4.5.1   *Scope of the development risks defence*

4.5.1.1 Background and nature   The Act provides a defence to a

s. 4(1)(e)   person proceeded against if he can show 'that the state of scientific and technical knowledge at the relevant time was not such that a producer of products of the same description as the product in question might be expected to have discovered the defect if it had existed in his products while they were under his control'. The term

s. 4(2)   'relevant time' refers in most cases to the time at which the product was put into circulation, and bears the same meaning as for the purposes of the subsequent defects defence, considered in 4.4.

The wording of the development risks defence does not follow that of the Directive, art. 7(e) of which states that the defence is available if the defendant can show 'that the state of scientific and technical knowledge at the time when he put the product into circulation was not such as to enable the existence of the defect to be discovered'. The formulation adopted by the Act has an interesting history. The version of the defence ultimately to pass into law was contained in the Bill as originally presented to the House of Lords, but that House inflicted a defeat on the government and substituted the wording of the Directive, their lordships being unable to comprehend why the government had thought it necessary to depart from what appeared to be the far simpler wording of the Directive. The government agreed to reconsider the matter, but nevertheless reinstated its own version in Committee in the House of Commons, apparently without the issue being discussed or voted upon. When the Bill was returned to the House of Lords for consideration of Commons amendments, objections to the reinstatement of the original formulation were reluctantly dropped, not on their merits but simply because Parliament was to be dissolved the following day and lengthy discussion would have resulted in the loss of the entire Bill.

The government's justification of its formulation of the development risks defence is that it more closely represents the intention of the Directive than does the actual wording of the Directive itself. This is a curious argument, for there is widespread acceptance that the version of the defence contained in the Act is wider than that in the Directive. Moreover, there would appear to be a number of significant difficulties arising under the Act which do not arise under the Directive.

(a)   Finding another producer who manufactures products of the same description is in most cases likely to be a theoretical exercise. Given that the development risks defence is almost certain to be confined to the supply of new products, it is likely that the defendant supplier possesses intellectual property rights which give it a monopoly position in the countries in which the rights are held. Consequently, unless licences have been granted or unless there are overseas manufacturers of the same product, there will simply not be any other person producing products of the same description with whom any meaningful comparison can be made.

(b)   The test in the Directive is objective, that is, it is concerned with the general state of scientific and technical knowledge. The Act, by contrast, refers to the subjective ability of some other, purely notional, producer to have discovered the defect. This leaves open the question: what are the deemed resources of that other producer? The answer determines the theoretical ability of that producer to have discovered the defect. There is some danger that the courts will compare the actual defendant with a notional producer of equivalent size and resources, and in this way introduce an element of subjectivity: the result might be that a small producer with limited resources might be able to escape liability simply because it did not have the ability to carry out all necessary testing.

(c)   The statutory defence, unlike that set out in the Directive, introduces a further complication in the concept of goods under the 'control' of some other notional producer. It is far from clear what is intended by this. Presumably the date at which goods cease to be under that producer's control cannot be the same as the date on which they were supplied (the 'relevant date'), as both concepts appear in the defence. One possibility is that goods remain within the control of a supplier after they have been supplied by him and until it is too late for him to recall them from circulation. How such a date is to be determined where there is no other producer actually in existence is, however, a matter of some difficulty.

It may of course be the case that the courts will seek to overcome these problems by looking beyond the wording of the Act and resorting to the phraseology of the Directive. However, if this does not occur, and the defence under the Act proves to be wider in its scope than that in the Directive, the issue will ultimately fall to be resolved by the European Court of Justice.

4.5.1.2   Effects of the development risks defence   The essence of the development risks defence is to permit a supplier to escape liability for putting into circulation a defective product which is in some way on trial, in that any defect was not, at the time of supply, discoverable under laboratory conditions. It is widely believed that the industries most likely to benefit are pharmaceuticals, in respect of undiscoverable side-effects in new drugs, and aerospace, in respect of design defects in aircraft: exemption for the former category is particularly ironic, for the Pearson Commission, which boosted the move towards strict liability for defective products, had been established in the wake of the thalidomide affair, but it appears unlikely that the victims of that drug would have been able to recover under the Consumer Protection Act 1987. The defence is not confined to the manufacturer of the product but is open to all persons potentially liable under the Act.

It may be seen that the broad effect of the defence is to incorporate into the Act what amounts to negligence-based liability, as the supplier is liable only where the defect was not discoverable by him. The burden of establishing the defence is, however, borne by the s. 3(1) supplier. The victim is thus somewhat better off under the Act than at common law for, rather than the victim having to establish negligence, it is the supplier's obligation to show that all possible tests had been carried out on the product.

4.5.2 Justifications of the development risks defence

4.5.2.1 EEC context   There was much debate in the discussions leading to the Directive about whether a development risks defence should be included in it. The problem stemmed from the fact that the pre-existing domestic laws of EEC member States had taken different views: some laws had imposed absolute liability either generally or in relation to specific products (notably, drugs) while others permitted development risks to be pleaded. The compromise adopted in the Directive is to include the defence (art. 7(e)), but to permit any member State to dispense with the defence in its own national legislation (art. 15, paras 1(b) and 2). In addition, there is to be reconsideration of the defence, in the light of decisions of national courts, in July 1995. Informed speculation points to the abolition of the defence in that year.

The attitude of the other member States of the EEC towards the development risks defence remains to be seen, but it is widely expected that the majority will take advantage of the derogation provided for in the Directive by not incorporating the defence into their laws. If this occurs, suppliers domiciled in other EEC States exporting products to the UK market will not face liability for development risk damage, although such liability might be faced on their domestic markets; this has led to fears that the UK might become the testing-ground for, in particular, new drugs. Moreover, it is far from clear that UK suppliers will receive any competitive advantage over their European rivals as regards exports to other EEC countries from the UK; while UK suppliers will receive exemption from liability in respect of supplies to the UK market, it is not certain whether the UK development risks defence will benefit them in proceedings brought elsewhere in the EEC. These matters are discussed in more detail in 6.2.

4.5.2.2 Innovation aspects   The most important justification of the development risks defence is that it encourages research into new products. The argument runs that a producer facing absolute liability for unforeseeable defects will simply not risk marketing new products, to the ultimate detriment of all consumers, because of the cost of potential liability from doing so and because of the danger of damage to reputation resulting from widely publicised successful proceedings.

The validity of the cost approach rests upon two assumptions. First, it presupposes that insurance will not be available for development risk liability. The preliminary view of the Association of British Insurers is, as already noted, that premiums will not be increased significantly by the imposition of strict liability as long as the development risks defence is available, but that there will be a substantial rise if absolute liability is imposed. Given, however, that insurance is available—albeit at a price—the question becomes whether it is proper to allow loss by development risks to fall upon individuals, or whether it is more desirable to require all consumers to contribute to the costs of insurance when making their purchases. The underlying assumption of product liability is that the latter option is the most desirable. It might also be questioned whether premiums would in fact have to rise as steeply as has been predicted by the Association of British Insurers: most of the calculations were done by assessing the American experience, although the high levels of damages there awarded and the contingency fee system may both render any comparison with the UK misleading.

The second assumption is that producers will not face development risk liability if a development risks defence is included. This, however, is not the case. First, an exporter to other member States of the EEC may, depending upon the conflict of laws rules prevailing in those States, face absolute liability. Secondly, the original producer may face liability in the UK under the Sale of Goods Act 1979, where a chain action is commenced. Finally, there is always the possibility that, following expensive litigation, the defence cannot be made out. Consequently, it would appear that UK suppliers would be unwise not to carry development risk cover irrespective of the position under the Consumer Protection Act 1987.

The reputation argument would not appear to be significant. In the absence of a development risks defence there would appear not to be a need for litigation, and all manufacturers would in any event face the same liability, so that there ought not be a fear of competitive disadvantage. In addition, reputation may be lost as much in successfully defending litigation as in accepting liability quietly.

4.5.2.3 Costs factors   The retention of a negligence-based inquiry within a system of strict liability may have important cost consequences. In establishing a defence, it will be necessary for the supplier to introduce much detailed evidence about the state of scientific knowledge at the date at which his product was put into circulation, thereby raising the spectre of lengthy and expensive trials involving conflicting expert testimony. This has significant consequences: many claims under the Consumer Protection Act 1987 will not be as straightforward as the principle of strict liability demands; and consumers may be forced, by the nature of the legal process in damage disputes, to settle for a sum not representing actual loss, as frequently occurs in negligence suits.

4.5.2.4 Deterrence It is arguably the case that the imposition of liability irrespective of development risks could bring about improvements in research techniques, possibly prompted by insurers.

Chapter 5

Scope of Liability

5.1 Foreseeability and Causation

The product liability Directive and the Consumer Protection Act 1987, unlike the common law, do not require for the establishing of liability that the loss suffered by the victim from the defect in the product was foreseeable. All that has to be established by the victim is that the defect in the product caused the loss. It should be stressed that it is not enough to show that the product contained a defect and that the victim suffered a loss from the product; the defect itself must be proved to be the cause of the loss.

s. 2(1)   The Act and the Directive express the causation requirement differently. Article 1 of the Directive provides that the producer is liable for damage caused by a defect in his product, and art. 8.1 stipulates that the producer's liability is not to be reduced when the victim's loss is caused both by a defect in the product and by the act or omission of a third party. By contrast, the Act states that there is to be liability in respect of damage caused *wholly or partly* by a defect in a product. The emphasised words do not appear in the Directive, and while they undoubtedly operate in the same way as art. 8.1 in imposing full liability on the supplier of a defective product even though a third party was partly to blame, it is arguable that they go further than the Directive in imposing liability where the proximate or dominant cause of the loss was an entirely natural event. The effect of the Act would seem to be that, where a defect in a product has any causal relationship with the loss, liability is imposed upon the supplier of the product unless it can be demonstrated that there was an intervening event which broke the chain of causation and which was solely responsible for the loss suffered by the victim.

5.2 Losses Recoverable

s. 3(1)
s. 5(1)   The Directive and Act are concerned only with external damage, that is, personal injury or death, and damage to the victim's other property, caused by the defect in the product. The Law Commission's

view that strict liability should be confined to personal injuries as opposed to property damage, given the availability of first-party insurance, has not found favour. Economic loss is not recoverable, nor is damage to the defective product itself. In the latter context, it s. 5(2) was noted in chapter 2 that the Act, unlike the Directive, does not impose liability upon the supplier of a defective component part for the damage caused by the defect in that part to the finished product.

5.2.1   Personal injury and death

The Act does not specify how damages for death and personal injury are to be calculated, and it may be assumed that the normal tortious measure is appropriate. Damages for pain and suffering are stated by art. 9 of the Directive to be recoverable if available under domestic law; this is the case in England. Where the victim has died as the result of personal injury inflicted upon him by a defect in a product, the Act preserves the rights of dependants and relatives to bring an action for damages under the Fatal Accidents Act 1976.   s. 6(1)(a)

Special provision is made to incorporate the provisions of the Congenital Disabilities (Civil Liability) Act 1976 into the strict liability regime. The 1976 Act confers upon a disabled child an action s. 6(3) against a tortfeasor in the event of an occurrence which affected the ability of either parent to have a healthy child (as long as neither parent had been aware of that fact) or which affected the mother during her pregnancy or in childbirth. The right of the child to bring an action is conditional on the ability of the affected parent to do so, but is not conditional on such an action actually having been brought by that parent. The Consumer Protection Act 1987 provides that where the parent has a right to sue for a defect in a product, the defendant faces the same liability towards a child suffering from disability following the parent's exposure to that product. It is anticipated that the most significant effect of the Consumer Protection Act 1987 in this context will be, subject to the development risks defence, to impose strict liability in respect of defective drugs supplied to either of the child's parents before conception, or to the child's mother during pregnancy or in childbirth.

5.2.2   Loss of or damage to property

5.2.2.1   *Property within the Act*   The Directive and the Act apply only to loss of or damage to 'consumer', as opposed to 'business', property, resulting from a defect in a product. Property may be either real or personal, and is within the Act if it satisfies two requirements:

(a)   it is of a description ordinarily intended for private use, s. 5(3) occupation or consumption; and

(b) it is intended by the person suffering the loss mainly for his own private use, occupation or consumption.

The formulation in the Act differs from the Directive in that the latter provides that the property lost or damaged must have been used in a private capacity, rather than merely intended for such use. The Act thus covers the possibility that the defective product has caused damage to the property in question before there has been any opportunity to use that property.

The use of the word 'mainly' in limb (b) of the test of 'consumer' property should also be noted. Property which has both domestic and commercial uses, but which is intended mainly for use in the domestic environment, is protected by the Act even if the damage was caused to it by the defective product at a time when it was being used in some commercial enterprise.

5.2.2.2 Date of damage

s. 5(5)

Ascertaining the date at which damage occurs is important for three reasons: it determines who has the right to sue, as only a person interested in property when it suffers damage has a cause of action in respect of that damage; it fixes the time at which the question whether the property is intended for 'consumer' or 'commercial' use is to be answered; and it marks the date at which the limitation period begins to run. Limitation is considered in 6.1, and the following paragraphs are concerned with the first and second of these matters.

s. 5(5)

The general principle adopted by the Act is that damage is deemed to have occurred when it first becomes discoverable. Consequently, the date of discoverability of damage to property determines who has the right to sue in respect of it and whether the property was intended for private use. The actual formulation used by the Act is, however,

s. 5(5)

rather complex. Damage is to be regarded as having occurred at the earliest time at which a person with an interest in the property (i.e., a person with a right to sue for loss or damage) had knowledge of the

s. 5(6)

material facts relating to the loss or damage. 'Material facts' are such facts as would lead a reasonable person to consider the loss or damage sufficiently serious to justify his instituting proceedings against a person who did not dispute liability. (This oddly worded test, which also applies to limitation, would appear to mean that loss or damage occurs as soon as the person interested in the property knew that it had suffered damage which was more than just

s. 5(7)

superficial or trivial; see 6.1.) Knowledge for these purposes consists of facts actually known by the victim, facts of which the victim ought to have been aware and facts which would have been discoverable by him had he acted reasonably and consulted an expert; in the last-mentioned case, if the victim has employed an expert, he is deemed to know only those facts actually discovered by that expert.

Some illustrations of these complex provisions may be of assistance:

(a)   Where property is of a description ordinarily intended for private use, and is intended to be used mainly for private use at the time of its loss due to the effects of a defective product, it is within the Act even though it had in the past been used primarily for commercial purposes.

(b)   Where a defect in X's product has caused damage to property belonging to A, and the property is subsequently sold to B, the action against X belongs to A if the damage was discoverable before the sale, and to B if it was discoverable after the sale. If the damage was discoverable while A was still the owner, B cannot sue for it unless A has assigned his right of action to B; in the absence of an assignment to B by A, B's rights, if any, are against A for either misrepresentation or breach of contract.

5.3   Financial Limits

5.3.1   Minimum loss

There is no minimum amount of loss required in order for a victim to mount a successful action under the Act for damages for personal injury or death. However, in respect of damage to property, damages are not recoverable under the Act in respect of loss or damage which does not, excluding interest, exceed £275. The purpose of this s. 5(4) limitation is, in the words of the ninth recital of the Directive, 'to avoid litigation in an excessive number of cases'.

It is not clear from the wording of the Act whether the sum of £275 refers to liability only in respect of property or whether it refers to the total liability of the defendant. Thus, if a defect in a product causes property damage to the extent of £250 and personal injury also to the value of £250, it is not clear whether the plaintiff can recover the total of £500 or whether he is confined to the sum of £250 representing his personal injuries.

5.3.2   Maximum loss

As a matter of theory, the maximum liability of a producer may be fixed in one of three ways. First, there may be a ceiling on the amount recoverable by any individual plaintiff. Secondly, the total amount recoverable by all plaintiffs in respect of a given defect in products marketed by the same producer and of the same description may be established. Thirdly, and by a combination of the above possibilities, each claimant may be subjected to a financial ceiling, with a further ceiling on the total amount awardable in respect of all claims for loss from the same defect in the same product.

The notion of a limit on the amount recoverable for individual claims has attracted little support: it is unfair to each victim, and it is not of assistance to producers as product liability insurance for single claims is often provided on the basis of unlimited liability or at a maximum level most unlikely to be reached in the ordinary course of events by a single claimant.

By contrast, the concept of a global maximum limit in respect of a defect common to goods of the same description produced by one producer has proved to have far greater support, mainly because the absence of a limit is believed to have an adverse impact on the cost of insurance or even on its availability. For these reasons the Directive, while not stipulating for any aggregate financial limit on liability, permits each member State to adopt the principle that 'a producer's total liability for damage resulting from a death or personal injury and caused by identical items with the same defect' is to be limited to an amount not less than £40 million (art. 16).

Nevertheless, the British government, following the firm recommendations of the Pearson Commission and the Law Commission on the issue of aggregate financial limits, has determined not to take advantage of the permitted derogation. The main reasons for this decision were as follows:

(a) It is impossible to fix one limit which is appropriate to all classes of goods.

(b) Potential defendants might be tempted to insure up to the limit of any statutory maximum liability figure, irrespective of whether that figure could feasibly ever be reached as a consequence of the harm done by any defect in the product in question; this would result in unnecessarily high insurance premiums and, therefore, higher ultimate prices to consumers.

(c) By imposing an aggregate limit, no individual claim could be settled until all possible claimants had been identified, in order to allow an equitable division of the sum available. This might in practice mean that no claim would be settled until the expiry of the 10-year long-stop for the issuing of proceedings, provided for in the Act.

(d) The amount of compensation available to each claimant might be artificially reduced in the case of a serious defect which caused widespread injury.

5.4   Exclusion or Limitation of Liability

The Act seeks to prevent a potential defendant from limiting or
excluding his liability towards the victim of a defect in a product. To
this end the Act provides that liability under the Act 'shall not be s. 7
limited or excluded by any contract term, by any notice or by any
other provision'. This protection is extended to claimants under the
Congenital Disabilities (Civil Liability) Act 1976 for loss within the s. 6(3)
Consumer Protection Act 1987: under the 1976 Act, a child victim
may otherwise be deprived of his rights by an agreement between his
parents and the wrongdoer.

There is, rather unfortunately, a serious drafting error in the
definitions section of the Consumer Protection Act 1987 which
appears to limit the efficacy of the prohibition on contracting out.
This concerns the word 'notice', which is defined as meaning 'a notice s. 45(1)
in writing'. The consequences of this definition would appear to be:
(a) that liability cannot be excluded or restricted as between plaintiff
and defendant by a contract term whether or not in writing (as there is
no rule of law which requires contracts for the sale of products to be
written in any way); but (b) that if there is no contract between
plaintiff and defendant, the defendant *may* exclude or limit his
liability by a notice which is not in writing (the word 'provision'
would appear to add nothing as, in its ordinary meaning, the word
surely implies something expressed in writing).

The reason for this peculiarity in drafting is found in Part II of the
Act, which deals with criminal liability for unsafe products. Various
of the enforcement powers there conferred upon the enforcement
authorities are exercisable by way of a 'notice' requiring particular ss. 13–15
action to be taken, and it was properly thought necessary to require
any such notice to be in writing. The definition of 'notice' is indeed
derived directly from that in s. 9 of the Consumer Safety Act 1978,
which Part II of the 1987 Act replaces. However, it appears to have
been overlooked that the word 'notice' also appears in Part I of the
Act, where it serves a very different purpose.

The point is further illustrated by the Unfair Contract Terms Act
1977, s. 2 of which renders ineffective any purported exclusion or
limitation of certain forms of liability, *inter alia*, by notice. The word
'notice' is there stated to include 'an announcement, whether or not in
writing, and any other communication' (s. 14). The same definition
would appear to be appropriate to Part I of the 1987 Act, and it may
well be that the courts will reach that conclusion in the face of the
clearly erroneous express wording.

5.5 Contributory Negligence

s. 2(1)   The supplier of a defective product is prima facie liable under the Act for all loss or damage caused wholly or partly by the defect. Where the loss or damage is caused partly by the defect and partly by a third party, the supplier remains liable to the defendant for the entire loss,

s. 2(5)   although he may seek contribution on a just and equitable basis from the third party. Where, however, the loss or damage is caused partly by the defect and partly by the contributory negligence of the plaintiff, the ordinary rules of apportionment for contributory

s. 6(4)(5)   negligence, set out in the Law Reform (Contributory Negligence) Act 1945, apply, and the defendant will be granted a reduction in damages proportionate with the plaintiff's degree of blame. The reduction is to be made in all claims, including those under the Fatal Accidents Act 1976 and the Congenital Disabilities (Civil Liability) Act 1976.

It is additionally possible that the plaintiff will be awarded nothing in respect of loss suffered by him from use of a defective product. This might occur, for example, where the plaintiff has put the product to a use for which it was not intended, or where he has disregarded safety warnings. In these and similar cases the defendant escapes liability

s. 2(1)   not because of the plaintiff's contributory negligence, but either

s. 3(2)   because the defect had not caused the damage or because the product satisfied the statutory test of safety and was not defective.

Chapter 6

Supplementary Matters

6.1 Limitation of Actions

6.1.1 General principles of limitation law

The English law of limitation, in so far as it applies to tort actions for personal injury and damage to property, is for the most part contained in the Limitation Act 1980 as amended by the Latent Damage Act 1986. Further amendments to the 1980 Act have been made by the Consumer Protection Act 1987 in order to incorporate the limitation principles of the product liability Directive. As will be seen, these are not in full accordance with pre-existing law and are to some extent rather less generous.

6.1.1.1 Personal injury claims An action in tort for personal injury and death must, in accordance with s. 11 of the Limitation Act 1980, be brought within three years of its accrual: the accrual date for these purposes is the date on which the damage occurred, whether or not the victim knew of his injuries at that time (*Cartledge* v *E. Jopling & Sons Ltd* [1963] AC 758). The difficulties that may be faced where injury does not become manifest until long after the expiry of the limitation period are overcome by the inclusion in s. 11 of an additional and alternative limitation period, which runs from the date at which the victim either knew, or ought reasonably to have become aware, of his injuries and of his right to bring proceedings. The test of knowledge and the facts which go to make up knowledge are defined elaborately in s. 14 of the Limitation Act 1980.

These time-limits are not, however, absolute, and may be extended in three cases:

(a) The court has a discretion under s. 33 of the Limitation Act 1980 to disapply the s. 11 limitation periods where it is of the opinion that their application would lead to injustice. The discretion is unfettered, is not confined to exceptional cases and is unlimited in the sense that there is no cut-off date for the exercise of the discretion.

(b) Where the plaintiff was under a legal disability (i.e., minority or unsoundness of mind) at the date of the accrual of his action, time does not run until the disability has come to an end. Section 28 of the Limitation Act 1980 here grants the plaintiff six years from this date to commence proceedings.

(c)   Section 32 of the Limitation Act 1980 provides that in cases of fraud by the defendant, of deliberate concealment of the right of action by the defendant and of mistake, time does not start to run against the plaintiff until he became, or ought with reasonable diligence to have become, aware of the fraud, deliberate concealment or mistake, as the case may be.

6.1.1.2   Claims involving damage to property   Negligence actions for property damage are governed by s. 14A of the Limitation Act 1980, as inserted by the Latent Damage Act 1986. Section 14A, like s. 11, provides for two alternative dates at which time is to start to run. The first is the date the plaintiff's action accrued, which is the date at which material damage occurred (*Pirelli General Cable Works Ltd* v *Oscar Faber & Partners* [1983] 2 AC 1); a six-year period is allowed here. The second date is that at which the plaintiff knew, or ought reasonably, to have known, of the occurrence of damage; three years only are allowed from this date. The meaning of knowledge and its elements are defined in s. 14A of the Limitation Act 1980 in terms similar to the definition in s. 14 for personal injury claims.

The limitation provisions for property damage differ from those relating to personal injuries in two respects. First, s. 33 of the Limitation Act 1980, which permits the court to extend time in personal injury cases, has no application to property damage cases. Secondly, s. 14B of the Limitation Act 1980, as inserted by the Latent Damage Act 1986, provides for a 15-year long-stop. The effect of s. 14B is that no action may be brought for property damage from a date 15 years after the date at which the defendant's last act of negligence to cause the defect in the property took place. In extreme cases, therefore, the long-stop might bar an action even before it has accrued. The long-stop is, however, overriden by the extensions of time available under s. 28 of the Limitation Act 1980 (legal disability) and under s. 32 of the Limitation Act 1980 (fraud, deliberate concealment and mistake).

6.1.2   Claims under the Consumer Protection Act 1987

6.1.2.1   Outline of the limitation provisions of the Directive   The time-limits for bringing actions, set out by the Directive, are somewhat tighter than those provided for by the general provisions of the Limitation Act 1980. The Directive establishes three principles:

(a) A basic period of three years, running from the date at which the plaintiff became aware, or ought reasonably to have become aware, of the damage, the defect and the identity of the producer (art. 10.1).

(b) A 10-year long-stop, running from the date at which the product was put into circulation by its producer, the expiry of which extinguishes all claims not commenced within that period (art. 11).

(c) National provisions which postpone the running of time are not to be affected by the Directive (art. 10.2) but are subject to the 10-year long-stop (art. 11).

6.1.2.2 The running of time under the Act The Consumer Protection Act 1987 inserts into the Limitation Act 1980 a new s. 11A, which provides for two alternative dates at which time begins to run. First, the plaintiff is allowed three years from the date at which his action accrues, i.e., the date at which personal injury or significant property damage was first suffered by the plaintiff. *s. 6(6)*

sch. 1, para. 1

Secondly, the plaintiff may bring an action within three years from the date of his 'knowledge'. The term 'knowledge' is defined by s. 14(1A) of the Limitation Act 1980 (as inserted by the Consumer Protection Act 1987) for the purposes of personal injury claims and by s. 14A for the purposes of claims relating to property damage. The definition has two distinct aspects: the meaning of knowledge; and the facts of which the plaintiff must have been aware. *sch. 1, para. 3*

It must be established that the plaintiff either knew, or ought to have known, of certain facts relating to his claim. The plaintiff is deemed to know such facts as were reasonably ascertainable by him or which could have been ascertained with the help of expert advice (e.g., medical advice in the case of personal injuries). However, where expert advice is taken and does not come up to proper standards, the plaintiff is not deemed to know facts which were not actually revealed by that advice; in short, the plaintiff does not bear the consequences of negligence by a professional adviser.

The facts of which the plaintiff must have been aware in order for time to begin to run are as follows:

(a) Facts about the damage that would lead a reasonable person who had suffered the damage to consider it sufficiently serious to justify his instituting proceedings for damages against a defendant who did not dispute liability and was able to satisfy a judgment. It would seem from these words that knowledge of even minor damage would suffice, as it would take little to persuade a reasonable person to sue a conceding and solvent defendant.

(b)   The fact that the damage was wholly or partly attributable to the defect.

(c)   The identity of the defendant.

sch. 1,
para. 1

6.1.2.3   Long-stop   The plaintiff's action is, irrespective of whether the time-limits set out above have expired, extinguished 10 years from the date at which the product was first put into circulation. This date varies depending upon whether the defendant is the producer, importer into the EEC or an own-brander, or whether the defendant is a mere supplier. In the former case the 10-year period for the long-stop commences at the date at which the product was first supplied by the defendant. In the latter case, the long-stop starts to run when the product was last supplied by the producer, importer into the EEC or own-brander. The date of last supply here refers to the finished product, and not to any raw materials or constituent parts incorporated into the finished product.

sch. 1,
paras 4, 5,
6

6.1.2.4   Extensions of time   The extensions of time available under ss. 28, 32 and 33 of the Limitation Act 1980 also apply to claims under the Consumer Protection Act 1987, although only claims for personal injuries are subject to the discretion of the court to extend time under s. 33. The scheme of the Consumer Protection Act 1987 is to allow the extensions to override the alternative three-year limitation periods in the usual way. However, the expiry of the 10-year long-stop established by the Act operates to put an end to all claims for which proceedings had not been issued, even though extension of time would otherwise have been available under the Limitation Act 1980.

6.2   Conflict of Laws

It is intended by the institutions of the European Economic Community that all member States will have domestic product liability laws corresponding to the Directive by the end of July 1988. The European dimension to the question of strict liability for defective products does, however, cause problems for both consumers and manufacturers in the United Kingdom. Two illustrations will be used in what follows:

(a)   A French manufacturer exports a defective product to England and causes loss to an English consumer.

(b)   An English manufacturer exports a product to France, and a defect in the product causes loss to a French consumer.

Three questions arise from these apparently straightforward cases:

(a)   Is the action to be heard in England or in France?

(b)   Wherever the action is heard, does the court apply English law or French law to the dispute?

(c)   Under what circumstances can a judgment, given in one member State in favour of a consumer, be enforced against a manufacturer who has no presence in that member State but who resides elsewhere in the EEC?

Issue (a) (jurisdiction) and issue (c) (recognition and enforcement) are governed by the Brussels Convention on Jurisdiction and the Enforcement of Judgments of 1968. This Convention applies throughout the EEC, although as yet not all of the member States have ratified it. The United Kingdom incorporated the Convention into domestic law by the Civil Jurisdiction and Judgments Act 1982, with effect from 1 January 1987. Issue (b) remains a matter of contention, in England at least.

6.2.1   Jurisdiction
The principle underlying the Brussels Convention is that a defendant is to be sued in the place of his domicile (art. 2). The term 'domicile' is not defined in the Convention but is a matter for domestic law: nevertheless, there is broad agreement amongst the contracting States that domicile in the case of an individual refers to residence and in the case of a company refers to either the place of its incorporation or the place from which it is centrally controlled and managed (for the United Kingdom, see the Civil Jurisdiction and Judgments Act 1982, ss. 41 to 43). Prima facie, then, in the above illustrations, the English consumer would have to sue in France and the French consumer would have to sue in England.

However, art. 5(3) of the Brussels Convention provides that in the case of matters relating to tort, delict or quasi-delict, proceedings may, in the alternative, be brought in courts of the place where 'the harmful events occurred'. This phrase has been held by the European Court of Justice, in *Handelskwekerij G.J. Bier BV* v *Mines de Potasse d'Alsace SA* (case 21/76) [1976] ECR 1735, to refer both to the place in which the negligence occurred and to the place in which the loss was suffered. Consequently, given that an action under Part I of the Consumer Protection Act 1987 is deemed to be one in tort for s. 6(7) jurisdiction purposes, it would seem that the French manufacturer in illustration (a) could be sued in either the English courts or the French courts, at the option of the English victim. In the same way, the English manufacturer in illustration (b) could well face proceedings before the French courts in respect of a defective product manufactured in England.

In most cases there will be no privity of contract between the parties, so that the above principles will govern the position. However, there may be exceptional circumstances in which a consumer domiciled in one member State has purchased the product directly from a person domiciled in another member State who faces strict liability for the defect in the product. Articles 13 to 15 of the Brussels Convention set out special jurisdiction rules for 'consumer contracts', a term which in the present context includes a contract for the supply of goods which was preceded by advertising and which was concluded in the State of the consumer's domicile. In such a case, the consumer may bring his action either in the courts of his own domicile or in the courts of the defendant's domicile. The position is thus the same as for actions in tort.

6.2.2   Governing law

Perhaps a more significant question is determining whether French or English law is to apply. In theory this ought not to matter, as the domestic product liability law of each member State should be the same. Nevertheless, it will be remembered that the Directive permits individual States some latitude on, for example, contribution rights and the assessment of damages, and the Directive also permits derogations in respect of maximum liability, agricultural products and the development risks defence. The situation might, therefore, arise in which the manufacturer would be able to plead the development risks defence if the matter was to be determined under English law, but in which the defence would not be open to him if the matter were to be decided under French law.

The rule prevailing in much of Continental Europe, including France, is that the law to be applied is the law of the place in which the wrongful act was committed. The English rule is less clear-cut for two reasons. First, a claim under the Consumer Protection Act 1987 is not deemed to be a tort for any purposes other than those of jurisdiction. Consequently, it is open to doubt how such an action would be classified by the English courts. Secondly, assuming that the action is classified as tortious, the law depends upon the proper interpretation of the baffling decision of the House of Lords in *Chaplin* v *Boys* [1971] AC 356. It would seem, however, that a tort committed in England is actionable in the English courts in the usual way, while a wrongful act committed abroad is actionable in England only if it was both actionable where it was committed and also amounts to a tort recognised by English law.

In order to establish which law to apply, the English and French courts in the above illustrations still face a critical question: in the case of a defective product manufactured in country A and causing damage in country B, where does the wrongful act occur—country A or country B? Such English authority as there is indicates that in this situation the tort is committed in the place of manufacture (*George Monro Ltd* v *American Cyanamid & Chemical Corporation* [1944] KB 432). If it is assumed that the position in France is the same, the results would be as follows:

(a)   (i)   A French manufacturer sued in the English courts is liable under English law, as the twin requirements of liability under both French and English law are met. As English law is to be applied, the French manufacturer has the benefit of the development risks defence.

(ii)   A French manufacturer sued in the French courts is liable under the law of the place in which the wrongful act was committed. If that is held by the court to be England, the manufacturer has the benefit of the development risks defence. If, on the other hand, the place of the wrong is held to be France, the development risks defence would not be available.

(b)   (i)   An English manufacturer sued in the French courts is liable under the law of the place in which the wrongful act was committed. If that is held by the French court to be England, the manufacturer has the benefit of the development risks defence. If, on the other hand, the place of the wrong is held to be France, the development risks defence would not be available.

(ii)   An English manufacturer sued in the English courts would be able to avail himself of the development risks defence even though his wrongful act was committed in France, as the requirement of liability under English law cannot be made out.

What emerges from the above is that the substantive rights of English manufacturers and consumers, engaged in litigation against persons elsewhere in the EEC in respect of product liability, rest upon a number of variables. These include: the extent to which different member States adopt different domestic modifications on the product liability Directive; and the conflict of laws rules of each member State as regards the applicable law and the place in which a wrongful act occurs. In short, the rights of an English consumer will vary depending upon where he sues, and the rights of an English manufacturer will vary depending on where he is sued.

6.2.3   *Recognition and enforcement*

The Brussels Convention establishes a uniform code for the recognition and enforcement of judgments as between Contracting

States. Under the Convention recognition is automatic (art. 26) and enforcement is a relatively simple process under arts. 31–49, resting on registration of the foreign judgment with the courts of the place in which enforcement is required.

Chapter 7

Background to Part II of the Consumer Protection Act 1987

Part II of the Consumer Protection Act 1987 is concerned with the safety of products supplied to consumers and of products used in the workplace. The latter is effected by amendments to s. 6 of the Health and Safety at Work etc. Act 1974. The former has a rather more complex history, which it is necessary to trace briefly in order to explain the shape of regulation adopted by the 1987 Act.

s. 36
sch. 3

7.1   Consumer Protection Acts 1961 and 1971

Statutory provisions regulating, through the criminal law, the quality of food, are of some antiquity. However, other products for a long time remained outside statutory control of safety, and the first attempt to bring the criminal law to bear upon suppliers marketing unsafe goods of other descriptions was the Consumer Protection Act 1961. This grandly titled statute was in fact rather limited in its scope and effects. The 1961 Act, as amended by the Consumer Protection Act 1971, was in essence an enabling provision, and permitted the Secretary of State to make regulations in respect of classes of goods to be selected by him, setting out such safety standards as were in his opinion necessary to protect the public against personal injury or death. Some 20 sets of regulations were made under the 1961 Act.

Nevertheless, the 1961 Act was found to have a number of serious weaknesses, which were outlined in a government consultative document on consumer safety, issued in 1976, Cmnd 6398. A major problem was the practice of basing regulations on safety standards established by manufacturers, as wide varieties of goods had not been rendered subject to agreed standards. Moreover, it proved to be a slow process to draft new standards and to modify or update the standards which had been established. Secondly, the degree of consultation between government and industry, which was a prerequisite to the making of statutory orders, led to much delay; the first 10 years of the operation of the Act saw only three sets of regulations brought into force. Thirdly, the enforcement authorities under the Act, local weights and measures authorities, were merely empowered—as opposed to obliged—to enforce the Act. Fourthly, not all forms of supply were covered by the Act; free gifts of unsafe goods were not, for example, regulated. Finally, and perhaps most fundamentally, the 1961 Act was concerned only with classes of goods specified by the Secretary of State in regulations; local authorities were powerless to act against goods falling outside those categories but which were patently unsafe.

7.2   Consumer Safety Act 1978

Many of the shortcomings of the 1961 Act were remedied by the Consumer Safety Act 1978, originating as a private member's Bill receiving government support, which was intended to replace the earlier legislation in due course. The main features of the 1978 Act were: a wider definition of 'supply'; the Secretary of State's powers to issue 'prohibition orders', 'prohibition notices' and 'notices to warn' in relation to goods governed by statutory orders; and a duty imposed on local weights and measures authorities to enforce the Act. The powers available to local authorities in enforcing the Act were also strengthened. A number of safety regulations were made under the authority of the 1978 Act.

Unfortunately, the 1978 Act also proved to be deficient, and was the subject of a White Paper entitled *The Safety of Goods* (Cmnd 9302) published in 1984. The most important weaknesses, and recommendations for their removal, identified by this document were the following:

(a)   The law was concerned primarily with the retail supply of goods and did little to prevent unsafe goods actually reaching the shops. It was thus necessary to improve the powers of enforcement authorities over imported products at their point of entry into the UK and to provide for the removal of goods from the market for a period of up to six months.

(b)   The law remained based upon the ability of the government to issue regulations concerning specific products, and that largely rested in turn upon the adoption of safety standards by the manufacturers of products. The solution would be the introduction of a general safety requirement applying to all products, which would exist alongside the specific regulations.

(c)   The improved enforcement powers conferred by the 1978 Act applied only to safety regulations made under that Act; the original regulations made under the 1961 Act remained governed by the more limited enforcement powers contained in that Act. Provision was therefore necessary for regulations made under the 1961 Act to be re-enacted under the 1978 Act.

7.3 Consumer Safety (Amendment) Act 1986

This Act, which was again in its origins a private member's Bill, implemented many of the proposals contained in the 1984 White Paper. The following were the most significant features of the 1986 Act:

(a) Customs officers were granted the power to detain for 48 hours imported goods suspected of being unsafe, to allow for their inspection by the enforcement authorities.

(b) The supply of unsafe goods could be suspended for a period of up to six months, either in the hands of their supplier or by seizure by the enforcement authorities.

(c) The power to forfeit unsafe goods, with the ultimate right to destroy them, was taken.

(d) Enforcement powers in general were strengthened.

7.4 Part II of the Consumer Protection Act 1987

Part II of the 1987 Act is a mixture of new provision and consolidation. The regime of safety regulations affecting individual s. 11 products is retained, in the improved form established in 1978 as amended in 1986. In addition, the Secretary of State now has the power to reissue under the 1987 Act regulations originally made s. 50(5) under the 1961 Act, incorporating such changes in them as he thinks fit. The best of the pre-existing position is in this way preserved.

The major innovation in Part II of the 1987 Act is the implementation of a general safety requirement. This requires all s. 10 consumer goods to be safe, and operates alongside the specific regulations: the general safety requirement and the safety regulations are collectively referred to by the 1987 Act as the 'safety provisions'. s. 45(1) Compliance with any specific safety regulations is deemed to be s. 10(3)(b) compliance with the general safety requirement.

7.5 Safety Regulations Predating the 1987 Act

It has been mentioned above that a number of safety regulations relating to specific goods had been made under the 1961 and 1978 Act. These are listed below. Those asterisked were made jointly under the 1961 and 1978 Acts. The government has stated that the earlier

Acts will not be repealed until steps have been taken to reissue under the Consumer Protection Act 1987 safety regulations made under them.

7.5.1 Safety Regulations made under the Consumer Protection Act 1961

Stands for Carry-Cots (Safety) Regulations 1966 (SI 1966 No. 1610).

Nightdresses (Safety) Regulations 1967 (SI 1967 No. 839).

Electrical Appliances (Colour Code) Regulations 1969 (SI 1969 No. 310).

Electric Blankets (Safety) Regulations 1971 (SI 1971 No. 1961).

Cooking Utensils (Safety) Regulations 1972 (SI 1972 No. 1957).

Heating Appliances (Fireguards) Regulations 1973 (SI 1973 No. 2106).

Pencils and Graphic Equipment (Safety) Regulations 1974 (SI 1974 No. 226).

Toys (Safety) Regulations 1974 (SI 1974 No. 1367).

Glazed Ceramic Ware (Safety) Regulations 1975 (SI 1975 No. 1241).

Electrical Equipment (Safety) Regulations 1975 (SI 1975 No. 1366).

Childrens' Clothing (Hood Cords) Regulations 1976 (SI 1976 No. 2).

Vitreous Enamel Ware (Safety) Regulations 1976 (SI 1976 No. 454).

Oil Heaters (Safety) Regulations 1977 (SI 1977 No. 167).

Babies' Dummies (Safety) Regulations 1978 (SI 1978 No. 836).

Perambulators and Pushchairs (Safety) Regulations 1978 (SI 1978 No. 1372).

Cosmetic Products Regulations 1978 (SI 1978 No. 1354).

Oil Lamps (Safety) Regulations 1979 (SI 1979 No. 1125).

*Cosmetic Products (Safety) Regulations 1981 (SI 1984 No. 1260), amended by *Aerosol Dispensers (EEC Requirements) and the Cosmetic Products (Amendment) Regulations 1985 (SI 1985 No. 1279).

*Nightwear (Safety) Regulations 1985 (SI 1985 No. 2043).

*Pushchairs (Safety) Regulations 1985 (SI 1985 No. 2047).

7.5.2 Safety Regulations made under the Consumer Safety Act 1978

Balloon-Making Compounds (Safety) Order 1979 (SI 1979 No. 44).

Dangerous Substances and Preparations (Safety) Regulations 1980 (SI 1980 No. 136), amended by Dangerous Substances and Preparations (Safety) (Amendment) Regulations 1985 (SI 1985 No. 127).

Upholstered Furniture (Safety) Regulations 1980 (SI 1980 No. 725), amended by Upholstered Furniture (Safety) (Amendment) Regulations 1983 (SI 1983 No. 519).

Novelties (Safety) Regulations 1980 (SI 1980 No. 958), amended by Novelties (Safety) (Amendment) Regulations 1985 (SI 1985 No. 128).

Filament Lamps for Vehicles (Safety) Regulations 1982 (SI 1982 No. 444).

Toy Water Snakes (Safety) Order 1983 (SI 1983 No. 1366).

Pedal Bicycles (Safety) Regulations 1984 (SI 1984 No. 145), amended by Pedal Bicycles (Safety) (Amendment) Regulations 1984 (SI 1984 No. 1057).

Motor Vehicle Tyres (Safety) Regulations 1984 (SI 1984 No. 1233).

Gas Catalytic Heaters (Safety) Regulations 1984 (SI 1984 No. 1802).

Food Imitations (Safety) Regulations 1985 (SI 1985 No. 99), amended by Food Imitations (Safety) (Amendment) Regulations 1985 (SI 1985 No. 1911).

Asbestos Products (Safety) Regulations 1985 (SI 1985 No. 2042).

Child Resistant Packaging (Safety) Regulations 1986 (SI 1986 No. 758).

Fireworks (Safety) Regulations 1986 (SI 1986 No. 1323).

Chapter 8

General Safety Requirement

s. 10(1)

It is an offence for any person to supply, offer or agree to supply or possess for supply consumer goods which do not conform to the general safety requirement. This chapter will consider the constituent

s. 41(2)

elements of the offence and the defences available to it. Breach of the general safety requirements does not give rise to a tort action for breach of statutory duty.

8.1   The Supplier

s. 46(5)

The Consumer Protection Act 1987 imposes liability only upon a person who is acting in the course of a business of his, whether or not his business is dealing in goods. The concept of acting in the course of a business is discussed in 16.2, and it is here sufficient to note that a person not in the business of supplying goods but who sells an item used in his business will not necessarily be subject to the general safety requirement, and that goods supplied in the course of a business of renovating and reselling will fall outside this part of the Act.

s. 46(7)(a)

Persons other than the supplier may also face liability. The circumstances in which this can arise are discussed in 16.4.

8.2   Supply

s. 46

The word 'supply' is given an extended meaning by the Act. This definition is discussed in detail in 16.1, but it may be noted that all

s. 46(1)

forms of transferring ownership in goods, whether by contract

s. 46(7)(b)

or by gift, fall within it. Supply of goods for their scrap value is, however, excluded from the general safety requirement.

Where the goods in question fail to comply with the general safety requirement, a supplying offence may be committed in one of three different forms:

s. 10(1)(a)   (a)   actual supply;

s. 10(1)(b)   (b)   offering or agreeing to supply;

s. 10(1)(c)   (c)   exposing or possessing for supply.

This broad wording overcomes the difficulty, encountered under earlier protective legislation, that a dealer who displays prohibited goods in his shop window cannot be convicted of offering to supply those goods (cf. *Fisher* v *Bell* [1961] 1 QB 394).

8.3 Compliance with the General Safety Requirement

8.3.1 Test of safety

In order to comply with the general safety requirement, goods must be reasonably safe. It will be recalled that for the purposes of Part I of the Act a product is unsafe if it poses a threat either of death or personal injury, or of damage to any property other than the product itself. However, for the purposes of Part II of the Act goods are safe only if they pose no risk, or a risk reduced to a minimum, of death or personal injury; potential danger to other products, and defects which render goods useless but not dangerous, are immaterial.   s. 10(2) s. 3 s. 19(1)

Lack of safety of goods for any reason contravenes the general safety requirement, although the Act specifies the various characteristics or uses of the goods which may render them unsafe: s. 19(1)

(a) the very nature of the goods;
(b) the keeping, use or consumption of the goods;   s. 19(2)
(c) the assembly of any goods which are not assembled on supply;
(d) any emission from, or caused by, the goods;
(e) reliance on the accuracy of any measurement, calculation or reading made by or by use of the goods.

8.3.2 Reasonable safety

It will be observed from the above definition that 'safety' is an absolute concept, in that a product which creates any threat of personal injury is unsafe. The general safety requirement is nevertheless satisfied if the goods are 'reasonably safe'. What amounts to reasonable safety is to be determined by the court taking into account all the circumstances, although the Act specifies three particular circumstances which must be taken into account.   s. 19(2)

First, the court must consider the manner in which, and the purposes for which, the goods are marketed, their get-up, the use of any mark in relation to the goods and any instructions or warnings given about keeping, consuming or using them. These factors are to all intents and purposes identical to those set out in Part I of the Act for determining whether a product is defective; for discussion, see 4.2.2.1. In the Bill as originally drafted the court was, in place of the above, required to take into account, for the purposes of determining safety under Part II, whether the product was defective under Part I.   s. 10(2)(a) s. 3(2)

However, the objection was raised that the court would be considering civil liability under Part I in order to fix criminal liability under Part II. For this reason it was thought wiser to reproduce separately what is in essence the same test in Part II, but tailored to criminal liability.

s. 10(2)(b)   Secondly, the court must consider any standards of safety published by any person for goods of the description in question or for matters relating to such goods. This is clearly intended to refer to safety standards issued by bodies such as the British Standards Institute and by trade associations. The use of the words 'published by any person' are curious, for they leave open the possibility of one or more manufacturers establishing their own safety standards, possibly based on irrelevant criteria, and declaring that their products comply with those standards. The government nevertheless decided that it would not be desirable to specify bodies whose safety standards should be taken into account, and was of the doubtless correct opinion that the courts are likely to give little weight to self-approval by manufacturers based on spurious criteria.

s. 10(2)(c)   Thirdly, the court must take into account the existence of any means by which it would have been reasonable to make the goods safer, bearing in mind the cost, extent and likelihood of an improvement in safety standards. This is perhaps the most important balance: is the cost of making goods as safe as is technically possible justified by the price that would have to be paid by consumers for those goods? It might, for example, be possible to improve the safety standards of microwave ovens but only at a cost which would force the price out of the reach of ordinary consumers. The way that this question will be approached by the courts is perhaps one of the most intriguing issues raised by the entire Act.

8.3.3 Deemed compliance with the general safety requirement
Consumer goods are deemed not to contravene the general safety requirement in four situations:

s. 10(3)(a)   (a)   where the allegedly unsafe feature is attributable to compliance with any enactment or any Community obligation;

s. 10(3)(b)   (b)   where the goods comply with specific safety regulations made
        (i) under s. 11;

s. 10(3)(b)   (c)   where the goods comply with standards of safety approved by
        (ii) safety regulations made under s. 11;

s. 10(3)(b)   (d)   where the goods comply with the requirements of any other
        (iii) enactment setting out safety standards for these purposes.

8.4 Consumer Goods

Consumer goods are goods ordinarily intended for private use or s. 10(7)
consumption. A number of items that would otherwise be consumer
goods are excluded from the general safety requirement. These are:

  (a) growing crops or things attached to land; s. 10(7)(a)
  (b) water, food (excluding tobacco, and as defined by the Food s. 10(7)(b)
Act 1984) and feeding stuff or fertiliser (as defined by the Agriculture
Act 1970);
  (c) gas supplied through pipes under the authority of the Gas Act s. 10(7)(c)
1986;
  (d) aircraft (other than hang-gliders but including gliders, s. 10(7)(d)
balloons and hovercraft) or motor vehicles (as defined by the Road
Traffic Act 1972);
  (e) controlled drugs (as defined by the Misuse of Drugs Act 1971) s. 10(7)(e)
or medicinal products licensed under the Medicines Act 1968;
  (f) tobacco. s. 10(7)(f)

The safety of these products is governed by other, specific legislation.

8.5 Defences

8.5.1 Due diligence
The Act provides a general defence of due diligence, which requires s. 39
the defendant to prove that he took all reasonable steps and exercised
all due diligence to avoid committing the offence. This defence is
discussed in 16.3.

8.5.2 Goods for export
It is a defence for the accused to show that he reasonably believed that s. 10(4)(a)
the goods would not be used or consumed in the United Kingdom.
The rationale of this defence was provided by the government in the
Parliamentary debates on the Bill: it is not the role of domestic
criminal law to protect the world at large; each nation must be
expected to develop and operate its own laws on the import of unsafe
goods; and requiring United Kingdom exporters to comply with
domestic United Kingdom standards, which may be higher than
those operating elsewhere, would be to put them at a competitive
disadvantage when vying with exports from other countries into
foreign markets. These considerations were thought to outweigh a
number of other factors: the notion of harmonising safety standards
within the EEC, a theme which underlies the product liability
Directive implemented by Part I of the Act; the possibility that

United Kingdom exporters as a whole might benefit from a general perception of safety, as opposed to the ability of individual firms to achieve short-term competitive advantage by exporting cheap goods not incorporating accepted safety standards (emotively referred to as a form of 'dumping' when practised by exporters to the United Kingdom); and the need to eliminate inadequate manufacturing and testing procedures from British industry.

The defence merely requires proof of the accused's reasonable belief that the goods were to be exported. Thus, the fact that products supplied by him do actually appear on the domestic retail market is not necessarily fatal to the defence. Where the accused obtained his belief from information provided to him by another person, it would appear that he must show that he took reasonable steps to verify that information (cf. s. 39(4)).

8.5.3   Retail sale

s. 10(4)(b) It is a defence for a person to show both: (a) that the goods were supplied, offered or displayed (as the case may be) by him in the course of a retail business; and (b) that at the date of the alleged offence he neither knew nor had reasonable grounds for believing that the goods failed to comply with the general safety requirement. This defence implements the view put forward in the 1984 White Paper to the effect that retailers are often not in a position to carry out detailed safety checks on goods supplied by them, and that criminal liability is more appropriately placed upon manufacturers and distributors. However, the implicit generalisation that all retailers are lacking in the sophistication necessary to test goods for safety themselves is probably as misleading as the assumption of the Act that all wholesalers are sufficiently sophisticated to do so. Large retailers who fail to implement safety checks may nevertheless be disentitled from relying on this defence by virtue of its second limb,

s. 10(4)(b) requiring an absence of reasonable grounds for believing that the
(ii) goods were safe.

s. 10(4)(b)   The definition of the phrase 'course of carrying on a retail business'
(i) sets out two requirements. First, the goods must be supplied in the
s. 10(5)   course of a business of making consumer goods available to persons who generally acquire them for private use or consumption. The fact that the particular sale in respect of which a prosecution is brought was not a consumer sale in this sense is immaterial. Secondly, the classes of goods supplied by the retailer in the course of his business must not to a significant extent include goods not previously supplied in the United Kingdom. The meaning of this is obscure, but would appear to exclude a retail business much of which consists of the supply of goods manufactured or imported by the retailer.

8.5.4 Second-hand goods

It is a defence for a person to show that the terms on which the goods   s. 10(4)(c)
were supplied, offered or displayed indicated that: (a) the goods were   s. 10(4)(c)
not supplied or to be supplied as new goods; and (b) the person   (i)
supplied or to be supplied would acquire an interest in the goods.   s. 10(4)(c)
   (ii)

The first limb of this defence raises two questions. First, when are   s. 10(4)(c)
goods 'new'? The courts have had to grapple with this issue in other   (i)
contexts, notably under the Trade Descriptions Act 1968 (*R* v *Ford
Motor Co. Ltd* [1974] 3 All ER 489), under the Sale of Goods Act 1979
(*Morris Motors Ltd* v *Lilley* [1959] 3 All ER 737) and in relation to
misrepresentation (*Raynham Farm Co. Ltd* v *Symbol Motor
Corporation Ltd*, *The Times*, 27 January 1987), but for present
purposes the correct approach would probably be to ask whether the
goods had ever before been sold to a business or private user. The
second issue is whether a supplier can take advantage of the defence
by advertising new goods as second-hand; this tactic is clearly
available on the wording of the section, which does not require the
goods to be second-hand but merely requires that they be advertised
as such. On the unlikely assumption that the defence would be
available in those circumstances, the supplier might well face
prosecution under the Trade Descriptions Act 1968 for applying a
false trade description.

The second limb of the defence seeks to exclude from its ambit   s. 10(4)(c)
goods supplied by way of hire only. To this end it is stated that the   (ii)
acquisition of an interest in the goods must be provided for or
contemplated in order for the defence to apply: goods sold either on
cash terms or by credit or conditional sale *provide for* the acquisition
of an interest by the purchaser, while goods supplied by way of hire-
purchase *contemplate* the acquisition of an interest by the hirer. The
purpose of excluding hired goods from the defence is to ensure that a
supplier carrying on the business of hiring out potentially dangerous
second-hand consumer goods, such as power tools and television
sets, is under a continuing duty to maintain them.

The exclusion of second-hand goods from the general safety
requirement has been justified on a number of grounds: purchasers
may be keen to purchase such goods in order to overhaul them; and
the imposition of stringent safety standards on the sort of retail
outlets which supply second-hand goods might well force them out of
business. It might be thought that these considerations do not
outweigh the need to protect the public against dangerous goods,
notably electrical products. However, the government has indicated
that the power to make safety regulations under s.11 will be used to
regulate the safety of certain classes of second-hand goods.

Chapter 9

Safety Regulations

9.1 Content of Safety Regulations

9.1.1 Scope and objectives of safety regulations

s. 11(1)
s. 11(7)
s. 19(1)
Safety regulations may be made by the Secretary of State in respect of all goods other than: growing crops and things attached to land; water, food (excluding tobacco and as defined by the Food Act 1984), feeding stuff and fertiliser (as defined by the Agriculture Act 1970); gas supplied through pipes under the authority of the Gas Act 1986; and controlled drugs (as defined by the Misuse of Drugs Act 1971) and medicinal products licensed under the Medicines Act 1968.

s. 11(1)
Safety regulations are to be made in order to secure the following matters:

s. 11(1)
(a) that safety standards are established or approved for the safety of goods;

s. 11(1)(a)
(b) that goods are safe;

s. 11(1)(b)
(c) that unsafe goods do not reach the market;

s. 11(1)(b)
(d) that goods which might be unsafe in the hands of particular persons or classes of person are not supplied to them;

s. 11(1)(c)
(e) that appropriate information is supplied with goods.

s. 19(1)(2)
The word 'safety' here bears the same meaning as is assigned to it in the context of the general safety requirement; see 8.3.1. This means in particular that safety regulations are concerned only with protection against death or personal injury, and not property damage or economic loss.

9.1.2 Making safety regulations

s. 11(1)
The Secretary of State may make such provision in safety regulations as he considers appropriate in order to achieve the above objectives.

s. 11(5)
s. 11(5)(a)
However, when he proposes to make safety regulations he is under a duty before doing so to consult such organisations as appear to him to be representative of interests substantially affected by the

proposal, and such other persons as he considers appropriate. s. 11(5)(b)
Further, where the proposed regulations relate to goods suitable for s. 11(5)(c)
use at work, the Health and Safety Commission must be consulted
(see further, chapter 12). The power to make safety regulations is s. 11(6)
exercisable by statutory instrument.

It will be noted that both the power to make safety regulations and s. 11(1)
the duty to consult interested persons before doing so are framed in s. 11(5)
terms of the Secretary of State's subjective beliefs. This wording
restricts challenges to the validity of safety regulations to those cases
in which it can be shown that the Secretary of State's belief that the
regulations were necessary, or that the proper persons had been
consulted, was so unreasonable that the Secretary of State could not
reasonably have held it (see, for a general discussion, *Secretary of
State for Education & Science* v *Tameside Metropolitan Borough
Council* [1977] AC 1014). The purpose of this limitation here is to
promote certainty about the validity of rules the breach of which
leads to criminal law sanctions. The subjective wording also makes it
virtually impossible for a person—assuming that he can demonstrate
a sufficient interest to commence proceedings—to claim that the
Secretary of State had not acted properly in failing to make safety
regulations or in limiting the scope of safety regulations.

9.1.3 *Matters which may be included*
The Secretary of State may provide for such matters as he considers
appropriate in safety regulations. The Act, without prejudice to this s. 11(1)
general discretion, sets out the types of provision which are open to s. 11(2),
the Secretary of State to include in regulations. The list provided by (3)
the Act may be divided into three classes: substantive, procedural and
regulatory.

9.1.3.1 *Substantive provisions* In broad terms, regulations may
either lay down minimum safety requirements or adopt safety
standards accepted by the manufacturers of given classes of goods.
The matters expressly referred to in the Act are as follows:

(a)   the composition or contents, design, construction, finish or s. 11(2)(a)
packing of goods, the standards for and other matters relating to the
goods;

(b)   requiring goods to be approved under the regulations or to s. 11(2)(f)
conform to the requirements of the regulations or to descriptions or
standards approved by or under the regulations;

(c)   the testing or inspection of goods, including the standards to s. 11(2)(g)
be applied in any test or inspection;

s. 11(2)(i)   (d) requiring a mark, warning or instruction or any other information to be put on or to accompany the goods, and securing that inappropriate information is not given;

s. 11(2)(j)   (e) prohibiting persons from supplying, offering to supply, agreeing to supply, exposing for supply or possessing for supply any goods and component parts or raw materials for those goods.

9.1.3.2 *Procedural provisions*   Safety regulations may provide for any of the following procedural matters:

s. 11(2)(b)   (a) the giving, refusal, alteration or cancellation of approvals of goods or of standards for goods;

s. 11(2)(c)   (b) conditions to be attached to any approval given under the regulations;

s. 11(2)(d)   (c) requiring fees to be paid on the giving or alteration of any approval under the regulations and on the making of an application for such an approval or alteration;

s. 11(2)(e)   (d) establishing appeals against refusals, alterations and cancellations of approvals given under the regulations, and against conditions imposed by approvals;

s. 11(2)(h)   (e) the ways of dealing with goods which do not satisfy a test required by or under the regulations, or a standard approved by the regulations.

9.1.3.3 *Regulatory provisions*   Enforcement provisions may be contained in safety regulations. The following are contemplated by the Act:

s. 11(2)(k)   (a) requiring information to be given to any person with enforcement functions under the regulations or Act;

s. 11(3)(a)   (b) requiring enforcement authorities to have regard to directions issued by the Secretary of State;

s. 11(3)(b)   (c) securing that the regulations are not contravened unless goods do not conform to a given minimum standard of safety;

s. 11(3)
(c), (d)   (d) determining that prosecutions shall be brought only with the consent of the Secretary of State or the Director of Public Prosecutions;

s. 11(3)
(e), (f)   (e) conferring jurisdiction on magistrates' courts to try an information if it was laid within 12 months from the date of the commission of the offence;

s. 11(3)(g)   (f) determining the persons by whom, and the manner in which, things required to be done under the regulations are done.

9.2 Breach of Safety Regulations

9.2.1 Civil liability

A breach of safety regulations is, unlike an infringement of the s. 41(1)
general safety requirement, capable of giving rise to an action in tort
for breach of statutory duty in favour of a person suffering loss as a
result of that breach. It should be borne in mind, however, that the
safety regulations are concerned only with the safety of goods in s. 19(1)
respect of personal injury or death; no duty is owed in relation to
damage to property or economic loss, so that damages for those types
of loss are not recoverable in an action for breach of statutory duty.
Moreover, the Secretary of State is empowered to include in safety s. 41(1)
regulations provisions limiting or excluding the right of an injured
person to bring proceedings in tort.

9.2.2 Criminal liability

9.2.2.1 Offences Safety regulations themselves cannot create new s. 11(4)
offences, and the extent to which infringements of safety regulations
amount to criminal offences is set out in the Act itself. It is, however,
necessarily the case that the number of offences which may be
committed under any given set of safety regulations depends upon its
terms. Four distinct offences are established by the Act.

(a) Where safety regulations prohibit the supply, offering or s. 12(1)
agreeing to supply, or exposing or possessing for supply, of any
goods, contravention of the prohibition is an offence.

(b) Where safety regulations require a person who makes or s. 12(2)
processes goods in the course of a business to carry out a particular
test on goods, and specify how goods failing that test are to be dealt
with, failure to comply is an offence.

(c) It is an offence to contravene a term of safety regulations s. 12(3)
which prohibits or requires the provision of particular information or
the use of a particular mark in respect of goods.

(d) Where safety regulations require any person to give s. 12(4)
information to an enforcement authority, it is an offence to fail
without reasonable cause to provide that information, or, where such
information is provided, knowingly or recklessly to make a statement
hich is false in a material particular.

9.2.2.2 Defences It will be seen from the preceding paragraphs
that the offences which may be committed under the safety

s. 12(4)   regulations do not, with the exception of (d) in 9.2.2.1, rest upon
s. 39   wilful or reckless conduct. It is a defence to offences (a), (b) and (c)
            for the accused to demonstrate that he took all reasonable steps and
            exercised all due diligence to avoid committing the offence. The 'due
s. 12(4)   diligence' defence is discussed in 16.3.

Chapter 10

Follow-up Powers

10.1 Outline of Available Powers

Four powers are available under the Consumer Protection Act 1987 to ensure that unsafe goods do not cause death or personal injury. These will be discussed in detail in this chapter, but it is necessary initially to outline their most important features as each power is exercisable in a different context, by different persons and in respect of different contraventions of safety law.

A *prohibition notice* may be served by the Secretary of State in respect of goods capable of being subject to safety regulations, preventing the supply etc. of goods to which the notice applies. s. 13(1)(a)

A *notice to warn* may be served by the Secretary of State in respect of goods capable of being subject to safety regulations and goods comprised in land, requiring any supplier of those goods to publish a notice warning that the goods are considered to be unsafe. s. 13(1)(b)

A *suspension notice* may be served by an enforcement authority where it has reason to believe that there has been a contravention of the general safety requirement, safety regulations or a prohibition notice. The notice may specify that the relevant goods are not to be supplied etc. for up to six months. s. 14

An *order for forfeiture* may be issued by a magistrates' court, on the application of an enforcement authority, on the ground of a contravention of the general safety requirement, safety regulations, a prohibition notice or a suspension notice. Forfeited goods may be either suspended from supply or, if necessary, destroyed. s. 16

One potentially important power which is not provided by the Act is that of recalling unsafe goods by way of 'recall notice'. Such a power exists in the domestic legislation of many other countries, but the government felt that it was both unnecessary, given the proven willingness of most manufacturers to recall dangerous goods voluntarily, and impractical, given that there would be no realistic way of imposing a recall requirement on retailers. Moreover, as will be seen in 10.3, notices to warn largely achieve the same aim.

10.2   Prohibition Notices

10.2.1   Scope of prohibition notices

s. 13(1)(a)   A prohibition notice may be served only by the Secretary of State, and only in relation to goods which are capable of being made the subject of safety regulations, i.e., all goods other than: growing crops or things attached to land; water, food, feeding stuff or fertiliser; gas supplied through pipes; and controlled drugs and licensed medicinal products. The power may be exercised whether or not safety regulations have been made.

s. 13(1)(a)   The effect of a prohibition notice is to prohibit the person to whom it is addressed from supplying, offering to supply, agreeing to supply, exposing for supply or possessing for supply, the goods specified in the notice. A prohibition notice may be less extreme, and may permit supply etc. with the consent of the Secretary of State subject to the

s. 13(3)   imposition of such conditions as the Secretary of State considers appropriate. The wording is subjective, so that the view taken by the Secretary of State of the unsafe nature of the goods, or of conditions to be imposed for permitting supply, cannot be challenged unless it is so unreasonable that it could not reasonably have been held by him.

s. 13(4)   Contravention of a prohibition order is a criminal offence.

10.2.2   Procedural aspects and appeals

s. 13(2)   The Secretary of State is empowered to make regulations specifying the manner in which information is to be given to the person upon whom the notice is served. The Consumer Protection Act itself sets out in detail the procedure to be followed in order to bring a prohibition notice into effect. The following are the salient features of the procedure.

sch. 2,   (a)   A prohibition notice must state that the Secretary of State
para. 1   considers that the specified goods are unsafe, set out his reasons, specify when it is to come into force and inform the recipient trader of his right to make written representations to the Secretary of State.

sch. 2,   (b)   On receipt of written representations, the Secretary of State
paras 2,3   may either revoke the notice or appoint a person to consider and report on the matter. In the latter event, the trader has a right to attend an oral hearing with the person appointed and to call witnesses.

sch. 2,   (c)   The person appointed by the Secretary of State must consider
paras 4,5   all of the evidence, both written and oral, and must report to the Secretary of State who may then revoke, vary or confirm the prohibition notice. Any variation may not, however, impose greater restrictions on the trader than the original notice.

10.3   Notices to Warn

10.3.1   Scope of notices to warn

A notice to warn may be served only by the Secretary of State, and in   s. 13(1)(b)
relation to any goods other than water, food, feeding stuff and
fertiliser, gas supplied through pipes, controlled drugs and licensed
medicinal products. A notice to warn may, unlike a prohibition
notice, be served in respect of growing crops and things attached to   s. 13(6)(b)
land. It is not necessary to the making of an order that safety
regulations affecting the goods in question are in place.
Contravention of a notice to warn is a criminal offence.   s. 13(4)

10.3.2   Procedural aspects and appeals

A prohibition notice comes into effect when served, although it may
be revoked following an independent report. By contrast, a notice to
warn must initially be served in draft, and the recipient trader has an
opportunity to require a report to be made before the notice comes
into effect. The procedure is broadly as follows.

(a)   Where the Secretary of State proposes to serve a notice to   sch. 2,
warn, he must in the first instance serve a notice on the trader which   para. 6
contains a draft of the proposed notice, states that the Secretary of
State considers that goods described are unsafe, sets out his reasons
and informs the trader of his right to make representations to the
Secretary of State.

(b)   If the trader does not, within 14 days, inform the Secretary of   sch. 2,
State of his intention to make representations, or if he fails to make   para. 7
written representations within 28 days, having stated his intention to
do so, the final notice to warn may be served. By contrast, if the trader
has made written representations within 28 days, the Secretary of
State must appoint a person to consider those representations and to
hold a hearing at which oral representations may be made and
witnesses called.

(c)   The person appointed by the Secretary of State must make a   sch. 2,
report for consideration by the Secretary of State; a final notice to   paras 8,9
warn cannot be issued until such consideration has taken place. The
Secretary of State may then withdraw the notice, issue it as originally
proposed or issue it in a modified form. In the last-mentioned case,
the modified notice to warn may not impose greater restrictions on
the trader than the original version.

(d)   Where a final notice to warn has been served, the trader
would appear not to have the right to have written representations
considered by the Secretary of State, although the Secretary of State
is empowered to revoke a notice to warn at any time.

10.4   Suspension Notices

10.4.1   Scope of suspension notices

s. 14(1)   A suspension notice may be served by an enforcement authority when it has reasonable grounds for suspecting that there has been—as opposed to a likelihood of being—contravention of a safety provision (the general safety requirement, any safety regulations or a prohibition notice). The notice may apply to any goods (other than those comprised in land and sold with the land) and its effect is to prohibit, other than with the consent of the enforcement authority, the recipient trader from supplying, offering to supply, agreeing to supply or exposing for supply the goods to which the notice relates for a period not more than six months from the date of service of the

s. 14(5)   notice. Any consent given by the enforcement authority may be
s. 14(6)   subject to conditions. Contravention of a suspension notice is a criminal offence.

s. 14(1)   The test for service is the existence of reasonable grounds for belief that a safety provision has been contravened. This objective wording indicates that a notice which is served in the absence of any reasonable grounds of belief is void. However, it would appear that the proper remedy in such a case is not an application for judicial review, but an appeal under the Act itself; see 10.4.2.

s. 14(1)   A further notice may not be served on the trader in respect of the same goods unless proceedings either for a breach of any safety provision or for forfeiture (see 10.5) have been instituted before the expiry of the original suspension notice. This type of notice is not, therefore, renewable unless other follow-up action has been taken.

s. 14(1)   The normal result of a suspension notice will be to freeze the goods in question in the hands of the trader; under the wide definition of 'supply' in the Act, a transfer of those goods by him will in most cases amount to 'supplying' them, in contravention of the notice. One exception might be where the trader rejects the goods under the Sale of Goods Act 1979 and restores them to the person from whom he received them; such a move does not appear to amount to 'supply' by

s. 14(3)   him. The Act also provides that a suspension notice may, in addition to preventing supply etc., also require the trader to keep the enforcement authority informed of any of the goods of the type in question 'in which he has an interest'. Generally, once goods have been supplied, the trader will have lost his interest in them, and it would appear that this further requirement is appropriate in two cases:

(a)   where the goods have been supplied by way of hire, lease or hire-purchase so that the trader retains title in them;

(b) where the goods have been supplied by way of conditional sale or under any other form of sale or agreement to sell under which property does not pass until full payment has been made by the purchaser.

A trader who has at the date of the suspension notice delivered goods to the buyer, but who has yet to be paid for them, no longer has any interest in the goods themselves, so that seemingly he cannot be required to reveal their whereabouts. In the same way, a trader who has rejected goods and has restored them to the person from whom he obtained them, would appear no longer to have any interest in them—at the most, he has an interest in restoration of the price paid by him, assuming that he is willing to part with the goods before he has been repaid—and is thus not obliged to inform the enforcement authority of his action.

10.4.2 Procedural aspects and appeals

A suspension notice must describe the goods to which it relates, set s. 14(2) out the grounds on which the enforcement authority has based its belief that a safety provision has been contravened and inform the trader of his right of appeal. Unlike the cases of a prohibition notice and of a notice to warn, appeal from the service of a suspension notice is judicial and not administrative. Any appeal is to be made to a s. 15(1), magistrates' court, with further appeal by any person aggrieved to the (2) Crown Court. The only ground upon which a suspension notice may s. 15(5) be overturned is that the court is satisfied that there has been no s. 15(3) contravention of any safety requirement in relation to the goods in question. One important question not dealt with by the Act is the burden of proving in appeal proceedings that the goods do not contravene a safety requirement, although this would seemingly rest upon the trader.

10.4.3 Compensation for wrongful service

Where, following the service of a suspension notice, it proves to be the case that there had been no contravention of any safety provision in relation to the goods in question, the enforcement authority is liable s. 14(7) to the trader for compensation for any loss or damage caused to him by the service of the notice. The Act appears to contemplate by its wording that such compensation is not simply calculated on loss of sales for the period during which the notice took effect, but may also cover any longer-term loss of reputation suffered by the trader.

Compensation is payable irrespective of the reasonableness of the conduct of the enforcement authority. An amendment to the Bill introduced in the House of Lords would have confined compensation to cases in which the authority did not have reasonable grounds for its belief, the purpose being to ensure that the authority was not deterred from acting where objectively there were good reasons to do so. This amendment was not, however, accepted. The only situation in which the trader is deprived of compensation is where his own default or neglect caused the authority to exercise its power to issue a

s. 14(8)   suspension notice. Any dispute about the level of compensation is to be determined by arbitration.

10.5   Forfeiture

10.5.1   Making an order for forfeiture

The ultimate sanction with respect to dangerous goods is an order for
s. 16(6)   their destruction. An order of this nature is available under the
s. 16(1)   Consumer Protection Act 1987 and may be issued by a magistrates' court on the application of an enforcement authority. Application to a magistrates' court for a forfeiture order may be made in the following circumstances:

s. 16(2)(a)   (a)   If the enforcement authority has brought proceedings in a magistrates' court in respect of a contravention of the general safety requirement, any safety regulations, a prohibition notice or a suspension notice, the authority may apply to that court for an order for forfeiture of the goods in question.

s. 16(2)(b)   (b)   If a suspension notice has been served by an enforcement
s. 15   authority, and an appeal has been made against that notice by the trader to a magistrates' court, the authority may apply to the court for an order for forfeiture.

s. 16(2)(b)   (c)   If a person interested in goods, which have been detained by
s. 33   an enforcement authority or by a customs' officer under their powers of enforcement contained in Part IV of the Act, applies to a magistrates' court for the release of the goods, the enforcement authority may apply to that court for an order for forfeiture.

s. 16(2)(c)   (d)   In any other case, i.e., where proceedings have not been brought in a magistrates' court, the enforcement authority may apply to a magistrates' court for an order for forfeiture.

s. 16(3)   An order for forfeiture may be made only where the court is satisfied that there has been a contravention of the general safety requirement, any safety regulations, a prohibition notice or a suspension notice. The trader, the enforcement authority and any
s. 16(5)   person aggrieved have a right of appeal to the Crown Court from the decision of the magistrates' court.

10.5.2 *Scope of an order for forfeiture*

Where it has been established that there has been a contravention s. 16(4)
of a safety provision in relation to goods from a particular batch or
consignment, or of a particular description, the Act declares that an
order for forfeiture extends to all goods of that batch, consignment or
description. This declaration overcomes the otherwise cumbersome
requirement for proceedings to be brought whenever there is a further
contravention of a safety provision in relation to goods of the class
forfeited.

Forfeited goods are to be destroyed in accordance with directions s. 16(6)
given by the court. However, the court has a discretion not to order s. 16(7)
destruction and instead to release the goods to the trader or any other
person specified by the court. The person to whom the goods are
released must, however, agree to two conditions:

(a) that he will not supply the goods other than as scrap or, where s. 16(7)(a)
he is in the business of repairing and reselling goods, other than in the s. 46(7)
course of that business;

(b)   that he will pay the costs and expenses of the trial and of the s. 16(7)(b)
enforcement authority in bringing the proceedings.   s. 35

Chapter 11

Enforcement of the Safety Provisions

 11.1 Enforcement Authorities

s. 27(1) The enforcement of Part II of the Consumer Protection Act 1987 is in the hands of local weights and measures authorities. The Act does
s. 27(2) provide for the transfer of functions, by the Secretary of State, to
s. 27(3) other bodies, but it is presently anticipated that the exercise of this power will be confined to transferring a limited number of duties of weights and measures authorities to the Health and Safety Executive. The Secretary of State himself plays no part in the day-to-day enforcement of Part II, although he does have the power to obtain the
s. 18 information necessary to exercise his own order-making powers under Part II.

The costs of enforcement are borne by enforcement authorities themselves. However, a person who is convicted of any breach of the
s. 35(1) general safety requirement, safety regulations, a prohibition notice or a suspension notice, or whose goods are ordered to be forfeited, may be ordered by the court to reimburse the authority for costs incurred
s. 35(2)(a) by it in connection with the seizure or detention of the goods or in
s. 35(2)(b) compliance with a forfeiture order. Reimbursement may also be ordered from any other person with an interest in the goods.

11.2 Test Purchases

s. 28(1) An enforcement authority has power to make any purchase of goods to determine whether any safety provision has been contravened. If
s. 28(2) goods purchased are submitted to any test, and the test leads to prosecution, the serving of a suspension notice or forfeiture, the authority must, so far as is practicable, allow the defendant or any other person with an interest in the goods to which the notice relates to have the goods tested.
s. 28(3) The manner in which the test conducted on behalf of the local
s. 28(4) authority is to be carried out is to be established by regulations. Existing regulations specify that testing is to take place at government testing laboratories. Some enforcement authorities have objected to

this, for the costs of testing are borne by them and they are of the view that independent testing laboratories might provide a cheaper service, but the government has adhered to the view that testing in approved laboratories removes all doubts in subsequent enforcement proceedings about the legality and reliability of testing.

11.3 Obtaining Information and Evidence

11.3.1 Powers of the Secretary of State
The roles of the Secretary of State under Part II are: (a) to make, s. 11
vary or revoke safety regulations; (b) to serve, vary or revoke a s. 13(1)(a)
prohibition notice; (c) and to serve or revoke a notice to warn. If the s. 13(1)(b)
Secretary of State considers that he requires information from any
person in order to decide whether or not any of these powers should
be exercised, he may serve a notice on that person requiring him to s. 18(1),
furnish the Secretary of State with the specified information. Failure (2)
to comply with a notice, or knowingly or recklessly submitting s. 18(3),
information which is false in a material particular, is a criminal (4)
offence.

11.3.2 Powers of enforcement authorities
The scheme of the Act is to permit officers of enforcement authorities
to inspect documents and goods in order to determine s. 29(1)
whether or not there has been a contravention of any of the safety
provisions set out in Part II. To this end the officers of enforcement
authorities are authorised to exercise any of the following powers at
any reasonable hour:

(a) to enter premises, other than purely residential premises;   s. 29(2)
(b) to inspect goods;   s. 29(2)
(c) to examine any manufacturing or testing process;   s. 29(3)
(d) to require the production of business records, take copies of   s. 29(4),
such records and seize and detain goods (including, where (5)
appropriate, breaking open containers or vending machines).

Goods and records may also be seized and detained where the s. 29(6)(a)
officer has reasonable grounds for believing that they may be
required as evidence in proceedings for the contravention of any
safety requirement. In addition, goods may be seized and detained if s. 29(6)(b)
the officer has reasonable grounds for believing that they are liable to
be forfeited. In both cases, containers and vending machines may be s. 29(7)
broken open to effect seizure. Where any goods seized are submitted
to a test, and the result of the test leads to criminal proceedings or to s. 30(6)
an order for forfeiture, any person with an interest in the goods is

s. 30(1) entitled to have them tested. In all cases in which goods or records are seized, the person from whom they are seized must be informed.

There will inevitably be cases in which enforcement officers will not be able to effect entry to premises in order to obtain information and evidence about contraventions of safety provisions. Consequently,
s. 30(2) the Act allows an officer to obtain a warrant from a magistrate, authorising entry to any premises, if there are reasonable grounds for
s. 30(2) believing either: (a) that goods or records which the officer has power
(a)(i) to inspect are on those premises and that they provide evidence of a
s. 30(2) contravention of a safety provision; or (b) that a contravention has
(a)(ii) taken place, is taking place or is about to take place on those premises. A warrant may be issued only where the magistrate is
s. 30(2) satisfied of any of the following: that admission to premises is likely
(b)(i) to be refused; that requesting admission would defeat the object of
s. 30(2) entry (e.g., that goods or records may be destroyed if prior notice is
(b)(ii) given); or that the occupier is temporarily absent and that the object of seeking entry would be defeated by awaiting his return. It would appear that a warrant may authorise entry to purely residential premises, a power which is not open to an enforcement officer in the absence of a warrant.

The Act sets out a number of offences relating to the obstruction of an enforcement officer. These are:

s. 32(1)(a) (a) intentionally obstructing an officer who is acting in pursuance of any of the above provisions;
s. 32(1)(b) (b) intentionally failing to comply with any requirement imposed by an officer acting within his authority;
s. 32(1)(c) (c) failing without reasonable cause to provide an officer with assistance or information which the officer reasonably requires for the purposes of the performance of his functions;
s. 32(2) (d) knowingly or recklessly making a statement which is false in a material particular.

11.3.3 Powers of customs officers

The consumer safety provisions apply equally to goods manufactured in the United Kingdom and to goods imported into the United Kingdom. It has nevertheless been recognised by the Act that the most effective protection against dangerous imported goods is to prevent them ever reaching the domestic market, and for this reason the customs authorities are given special powers. These are twofold.

First, the Commissioners of Customs and Excise may, if they think   s. 37(it appropriate to do so for the purpose of facilitating an enforcement authority in the exercise of its functions, disclose to the authority any

information obtained by them in the course of their duties and s. 37(2)
powers in relation to imported goods. Any such information may be s. 37(4)
volunteered; a request by the authority is not required.

Secondly, a customs officer may, for the purpose of facilitating an s. 31(1)
enforcement authority in the exercise of its powers, seize any
imported goods and detain them for not more than two working
days. Following such seizure, the enforcement authority is able to
make a preliminary examination of the goods to determine whether
they appear to contravene any safety provision. In the Bill as
originally drafted, only 48 hours was allowed for this process. This
provoked the criticism that it might have been difficult for an
adequate examination to be arranged within that period, particularly
during a weekend or public holiday period, and that detention for a
period up to one week would have been more appropriate. The
government ultimately compromised by amending the 48-hour
period to two working days, thereby overcoming the weekend s. 31(2)
and public holiday problems. Arguments for an even longer period
were, however, rejected on a number of grounds:

(a)   The purpose of the procedure is not to facilitate a full inquiry,
including testing, but merely to allow the authority to make
preliminary inquiries.

(b)   An enforcement authority which has severe doubts about the
safety of imported goods may serve a suspension notice, preventing
their supply for up to six months. The problem here, however, is that
if it is subsequently shown that the goods do not contravene any
safety provision, the authority will normally be liable to compensate
any person with an interest in the goods who has suffered loss by their
detention. It is thus feared that enforcement authorities might be
prepared to allow 'dubious' goods on to the market and thereafter to
make closer examination of them, rather than to face the risk of
having to pay compensation following a snap decision.

(c)   Any longer period of detention might be perceived by the
European Commission as disguised discrimination against imported
goods and thus contrary to the free movement of goods provisions of
art. 30 of the Treaty of Rome.

It is a criminal offence intentionally to obstruct a customs officer
who is acting in the course of his functions under the Act.

11.3.4   Restrictions on disclosure of information

It is a criminal offence for any person to disclose information s. 38(1)
obtained by him as a result of the operation of the enforcement s. 38(5)
procedures of the Act. There are nevertheless exceptions to this

general principle, which permit disclosure in the following circumstances:

s. 38(2)   (a)   If the information has previously been published, by virtue of
s. 38(6)   civil or criminal proceedings or having been included in a notice to warn.
s. 38(2)(a)   (b)   For the purpose of facilitating the exercise of functions under
s. 38(4)   the Consumer Protection Act 1987 itself and under a number of other
s. 38(3)   pieces of consumer protection legislation, notably the Trade Descriptions Act 1968, the Fair Trading Act 1973 and competition legislation generally.
s. 38(2)(b)   (c)   For the purpose of compliance with a Community obligation.
s. 38(2)(c)   (d)   In connection with the investigation of any criminal offence and for the purposes of any civil or criminal proceedings.

11.4   Seizure and Detention of Goods

11.4.1   Grounds for seizure and detention
Goods may be seized by enforcement authorities on a number of grounds under the Act:

s. 29(4)(b)   (a)   ascertaining the safety of goods not previously supplied in the United Kingdom;
s. 29(5)(b)   (b)   determining whether a safety provision has been contravened;
s. 29(6)(a)   (c)   as evidence of the commission of an offence against the safety provisions of the Act;
s. 29(6)(b)   (d)   where the goods are suspected of being liable to forfeiture under a forfeiture order.

11.4.2   Appeals against seizure and detention
s. 33(1)   Any person having an interest in goods for the time being detained by an enforcement authority may apply to a magistrates' court for an
s. 33(2)(a)   order requiring the goods to be released to him or to another person. If criminal proceedings have been brought, or forfeiture has been applied for, application for release is to be made to the magistrates'
s. 33(2)(b)   court concerned with the matter; where there are no proceedings, application may be made to any magistrates' court.

     Release is to be ordered only where the magistrates' court is
s. 33(3)(b)   satisfied either: (a) that no proceedings have been brought for infringement of any safety provision or for forfeiture, and that six
s. 33(3)(a)   months have elapsed since the date of seizure; or (b) that proceedings for infringement or forfeiture have been brought and concluded without an order for forfeiture being made. By this means the Act, in

effect, requires enforcement proceedings to be brought within six months from the date of seizure of any goods. Appeal may be made by any person aggrieved to the Crown Court. s. 33(4)

11.4.3 Compensation for seizure and detention

Where goods have been seized and detained, and it subsequently proves to be the case that no offence against any safety provision had been committed, any person with an interest in the goods is entitled to compensation for any resulting loss or damage to him. This may apparently include loss of reputation as well as loss of profit. Any dispute about the amount of compensation payable is to be determined by arbitration. The right to compensation is lost only where the seizure or detention of the goods was in some way attributable to the neglect of the person seeking compensation. The good faith of the enforcement authority, and the strength of the evidence on which seizure took place, do not affect the right of compensation. s. 34(1)
s. 34(1)(a)
s. 34(2)
s. 34(1)(b)

The Act awards compensation only where 'there has been no contravention'. Consequently it would appear that compensation is not available where goods have been seized and detained for a period exceeding six months without proceedings being commenced and a person interested in them has obtained their release from a magistrates' court. s. 34(1)(a)

11.5 Proceedings

Criminal proceedings in relation to the infringement of any safety provision may be initiated only by enforcement authorities. Civil proceedings, by way of action for breach of statutory duty, are available for an infringement of any safety regulations. However, there is no civil remedy under the Act for breach of the general safety requirement, a prohibition notice or a suspension notice. Where there is civil liability, it may not be limited or excluded by any contract term or notice. 'Notice' means 'notice in writing', so that taken literally the Act permits the limitation or exclusion of non-contractual liability by oral notification. An explanation for this oddity was proffered in 5.4. s. 27
s. 41(1)
s. 41(2)
s. 41(4)

An agreement is not, subject to its own terms, void or unenforceable as a result of the contravention of any safety provision. s. 41(3)

Chapter 12

Safety of Goods and Substances at Work

12.1 Regulatory Structure

12.1.1 Scope of Health and Safety at Work etc. Act 1974

Part I of the Health and Safety at Work etc. Act 1974 (HSWA 1974) sets out a complex regulatory structure for securing the health, safety and welfare of persons at work. The controls are in two forms. First, general duties of care are imposed upon employers, in relation to employees (s. 2) and self-employed persons (s. 3), upon suppliers of goods and substances for use at work (s. 6) and upon employees themselves (s. 7). Secondly, health and safety regulations and codes of practice are issued respectively by the Secretary of State and the Health and Safety Commission under ss. 15 and 16, governing particular aspects of health and safety at the workplace. Enforcement of the law is primarily in the hands of the Health and Safety Executive, which works under the general guidance of the Commission. Enforcement is mainly by criminal proceedings; a person injured by a breach of the general duties is not granted an action for breach of statutory duty, although such an action is available in respect of breaches of health and safety regulations (s. 47).

12.1.2 Impact of Consumer Protection Act 1987

s. 36

The 1987 Act seeks to establish common principles, as far as is appropriate, for the safety of consumer goods generally and for the safety of goods and substances for use at work. Consequently, the Act

sch. 3

makes a number of small but significant amendments to s. 6 of the HSWA 1974, and also strengthens the enforcement powers of the Executive in line with the powers granted to local authorities under Part II of the 1987 Act. The most important modifications of the HSWA 1974 introduced by the 1987 Act may be summarised as follows:

sch. 3,
para. 1
sch. 3,
para. 1

(a)   Section 6 is extended to cover fairground equipment.

(b)   Section 6 in its original form was concerned with the safety of goods and substances only in respect of their use, whereas s. 6 as amended extends the safety requirement to the setting, cleaning and maintenance of goods and the handling, processing, storing and transporting of substances.

(c)   It was unclear under the old s. 6 whether instructions had to be provided by the supplier of an item or substance or merely had to be made available by him—the amendments make it clear that the former, stricter, duty applies and that revisions of information in the light of any discovery of new threats to health or safety must be communicated.

sch. 3, para. 1

(d)   Powers are conferred upon the Commissioners of Customs and Excise to detain imported goods and to provide information to the Executive.

sch. 3, paras 3–6

(e)   The safety provisions are extended to the supply of micro-organisms.

sch. 3, para. 7

12.2   Duties in Relation to Goods and Substances

The duties imposed by s. 6 of the HSWA 1974, as amended by the Consumer Protection Act 1987, are outlined in this section. In all cases liability attaches only to a person acting within the course of a trade or business and to matters within his control (HSWA 1974, s. 6(7)). However, an importer remains liable even though the risks to health and safety resulted from manufacture or design outside his control (HSWA 1974, s. 6(8A)).

sch. 3, para. 1

12.2.1   Goods for use at work

Four distinct duties, enforceable under the criminal law only, are imposed by s. 6(1) of the HSWA 1974 upon any person who designs, manufactures, imports or supplies any article for use at work. An article for use at work is any machinery, equipment or appliance designed for use or operation (whether exclusively or not) by persons at work and any article designed for use as a component (HSWA 1974, s. 53(1)). Supply may be by means of sale, lease, hire or hire-purchase (HSWA 1974, s. 53(1)), although where the supplier in law is a financing organisation rather than a dealer (e.g., under a typical hire-purchase arrangement), liability attaches to the dealer alone (HSWA 1974, s. 6(9); cf. s. 46(2) of the 1987 Act).

The duties imposed by s. 6(1), echoed in s. 6(1A) in respect of fairground equipment, are as follows:

sch. 3, para. 1

(a)   To ensure, whether by information, advice or otherwise and so far as is reasonably practicable, that the article is so designed and constructed that it will be safe and without risks to health at all times when it is being set, used, cleaned or maintained by a person at work. This duty may be shifted on to another person by virtue of an agreement in writing whereby that other undertakes to ensure that the article will be safe and without risks to health (HSWA 1974, s. 6(8)).

(b)   To carry out or arrange for the carrying out of such testing and examination as may be necessary for the performance of the duty in (a) above.

(c)   To take such steps as are necessary to secure that persons supplied with the article are also provided with adequate information about the use for which the article is designed or has been tested, and about any conditions necessary to ensure that it will be safe and without risks to health when it is being set, used, cleaned, maintained, dismantled or disposed of by a person at work.

(d)   To take such steps as are necessary to secure, so far as is reasonably practicable, that persons supplied are provided with all relevant revisions of information when it becomes known that the article gives rise to a serious risk to health or safety.

Risks to health or safety which cannot reasonably be foreseen are to be disregarded (HSWA 1974, s. 6(10)).

12.2.2   Safety research into articles by designer or manufacturer

sch. 3,
para. 1

It is the duty of any person who designs or manufactures any article for use at work, or any fairground equipment, to carry out or arrange for the carrying out of any research necessary: (a) to discover any risks to health and safety to which the article or its design may give rise; and (b) to minimise or eliminate any risk (HSWA 1974, s. 6(2)).

12.2.3   Erection or installation of articles for use at work

sch. 3,
para. 1

It is the duty of any person who erects or installs any article for use at work, or any fairground equipment, to ensure, so far as is reasonably practicable, that nothing about its erection or installation makes it unsafe or a risk to health when it is being set, used, cleaned or maintained (HSWA 1974, s. 6(3)).

12.2.4   Substances for use at work

Four duties, analogous to those in HSWA 1974, s. 6(1), in relation to goods, are set out by HSWA 1974, s. 6(4), in respect of the manufacture, import or supply of substances used at work. A substance for use at work is any natural or artificial substance, including micro-organisms, whether in solid or liquid form or in the form of a gas or vapour which is intended for use (whether exclusively or not) by persons at work (HSWA 1974, s. 53(1)).

The duties imposed by HSWA 1974, s. 6(4), are as follows:

sch. 3,
para. 1

(a)   To ensure, whether by information, advice or otherwise and so far as is reasonably practicable, that the substance will be safe and without risks at all times when it is being used, handled, processed, stored or transported by a person at work or on non-domestic premises.

(b)   To carry out or arrange for the carrying out of such testing and examination as may be necessary for the performance of the duty in (a) above.

(c)   To take such steps as are necessary to secure that persons supplied with the substance are provided with adequate information about any risks to health or safety to which the inherent properties of the substance may give rise, about the results of any relevant tests which have been carried out and about any conditions necessary to ensure that the substance will be safe and without risks to health when it is being used, handled, processed, stored, transported or disposed of.

(d)   To take such steps as are necessary to secure, so far as is reasonably practicable, that persons supplied are provided with all relevant revisions of information when it becomes known that the substance gives rise to a serious risk to health or safety.

12.2.5   *Safety research into substances by manufacturer*
It is the duty of any person who maufactures any substance to carry out or arrange for the carrying out of any research necessary: (a) to discover any risks to health and safety to which the substance may give rise; and (b) to minimise or eliminate any risk (HSWA 1974, s. 6(5)). *sch. 3, para. 1*

12.3   Enforcement

12.3.1   *Powers of the enforcement authorities*

12.3.1.1   Role of inspectors   Enforcement is primarily the task of the Health and Safety Executive, and is carried out by appointed inspectors (HSWA 1974, ss. 19 and 20), who are given powers of entry, search and seizure of samples (HSWA 1974, s. 20).

12.3.1.2   Notices   An inspector may serve improvement or prohibition notices (HSWA 1974, ss. 21 to 23). The former notice specifies a contravention of the Act and requires remedial action within the period stated in the notice. The latter type of notice may be served in relation to activities which are, or are likely to be, carried on in breach of the Act, and prohibits such activities; a prohibition notice may take effect immediately or after such period as may be stated in the notice. *sch. 3, para. 2*

12.3.1.3   Seizure of offending articles and substances   Seizure may
take place in two circumstances. First, where an inspector has
reasonable cause to believe that an article or substance is a cause of
imminent danger or serious personal injury, it may be seized and

sch. 3,   rendered harmless, if necessary by destruction (HSWA 1974, s. 25).
para. 3   Secondly, a customs officer may, in order to facilitate the exercise of
an inspector's powers, detain any imported article or substance for up
to two working days (HSWA 1974, s. 25A). This power was inserted
by the Consumer Protection Act 1987, and is the counterpart of s. 31
of the 1987 Act.

12.3.2   Obtaining and disclosure of information

The Executive is empowered to obtain such information as it needs
for the discharge of its functions (HSWA 1974, s. 27). Moreover, the

sch. 3,   Commissioners of Customs and Excise may authorise disclosure to
para. 4   the Executive of information relevant to the Executive's functions
and obtained in connection with imports (HSWA 1974, s. 27A); this
power was added by the Consumer Protection Act 1987, and is the
counterpart of s. 37 of the 1987 Act. Information provided to the

sch. 3,   Executive must not be disclosed by it without the consent of the
para. 5   person who provided it (HSWA 1974, s. 28).

12.3.3   Offences

A number of offences are set out in HSWA 1974, s. 33. Those
relevant for present purposes include: failure to discharge any of the
duties established by HSWA 1974, s. 6; contravention of any
requirement imposed by an inspector in relation to search and to
removal of products which are an immediate threat to safety; breach

sch. 3,   of an improvement or prohibition notice; and obstruction of an
para. 6   inspector or customs officer in the exercise of their duties.

Chapter 13

Background to the Misleading Pricing Provisions

13.1 Statutory Framework

Before the passing of the Consumer Protection Act 1987 there was no single offence of giving a misleading price indication. Rather, there were two pieces of legislation—one primary and one subordinate—which sought to control this problem. The first was s.11 of the Trade Descriptions Act 1968, which was aimed at retailers and which outlawed three specific classes of false or misleading statements relating to the price of goods. Each of these offences was of strict liability,and was restricted to a person acting in the course of a trade or business (*John* v *Matthews* [1970] 2 QB 443). Secondly, the Price Marking (Bargain Offers) Order 1979 (SI 1979 No. 364), as amended by SIs 1979 Nos. 633 and 1124, prohibited specified price comparisons regarded as misleading in themselves: the critical difference between the Order and s. 11 was that liability under the Order did not depend upon proof that the comparison was false, but rested simply on the fact that a prohibited comparison had been made.

The purpose of this chapter is to outline the pre-existing provisions and to highlight their deficiencies, by way of setting the scene for discussion of the new offence of giving a misleading price indication.

13.2 Section 11 of the Trade Descriptions Act 1968

13.2.1 False comparisons between actual prices and recommended prices
It was an offence to give an indication that goods were being offered for sale at less than their recommended price, which was assumed to be the manufacturers' recommended price unless the contrary was stated (Trade Descriptions Act 1968, s. 11(1)(a)). Such prosecutions as were brought were founded on clerical errors (e.g., *Butler* v *Keenway Supermarkets Ltd* [1974] Crim LR 560; *McGuire* v

Sittingbourne Co-operative Society Ltd [1976] Crim LR 268). However, the Act did not address a series of difficulties: manufacturers' recommended prices often bear no relation to the anticipated reselling price, and permit misleadingly favourable comparisons to be advertised by retailers; it was open to a retailer to compare his price with any manufacturer's recommended price, whether or not it was current and applicable to the retailer's own locality; and retailers remained free to establish their own recommended prices and advertise reductions against those.

13.2.2   *False comparisons between previous and existing prices*
It was an offence for a person to give a false indication of the price at which goods had previously been sold by him (Trade Descriptions Act 1968, s. 11(1)(b)). The drafting of this provision, coupled with some curious judicial decisions, resulted in a number of weaknesses becoming apparent:

(a)   The criterion by which price reductions could be advertised— that the goods had been offered at a higher price for 28 consecutive days in the preceding six months—was almost inevitably construed as meaning that price fluctuations following those 28 days but within the preceding six months could be disregarded. Thus goods sold at £20 for 28 days and at £15 for the following five months could legitimately be advertised thereafter at £18 reduced from £20 (*House of Holland Ltd* v *Brent London Borough Council* [1971] 2 QB 304).

(b)   Comparisons could be made as between branches within the same store chain. Thus, a retailer who sold goods at £10 in branch A and at £12 in branch B, could raise the price in branch A to £11 and advertise the goods as reduced from £12 (*Westminster City Council* v *Ray Alan (Manshops) Ltd* [1982] 1 All ER 771).

(c)   Vague claims which did not give any indication of an earlier price but which nevertheless suggested that a reduction had taken place were lawful: on this basis the Act exempted bogus 'closing-down sales' (*Westminster City Council* v *Ray Alan (Manshops) Ltd* [1982] 1 All ER 771), 'extra value' and 'worth' claims (*Cadbury Ltd* v *Halliday* [1975] 2 All ER 226), 'now only' claims and the use of inferior quality goods not previously marketed, in seasonal 'sales'.

(d)   False comparisons with the prices of other retailers were not unlawful.

(e)   It was permissible to advertise goods at bargain prices, in order to attract customers to the premises, when in fact stocks of those goods were not held.

13.2.3   Misstatement of actual price

It was an offence for a person to give any indication that goods were being offered at a price less than their actual price (Trade Descriptions Act 1968, s. 11(2)). This was the closest thing to a general offence of misleading pricing in the 1968 Act, and proved to be effective against, *inter alia*, price indications which omitted additional charges (*Richards* v *Westminster Motors Ltd* [1976] RTR 88), erroneous price labels on goods (*Tesco Supermarkets Ltd* v *Nattrass* [1972] AC 153; *Doble* v *David Greig Ltd* [1972] 2 All ER 195) and offers of discounts which did not accurately state the goods to which they applied (*North Western Gas Board* v *Aspden* [1970] Crim LR 301).

A number of uncertainties about the scope of s. 11(2) subsequently became apparent. These included:

(a)   Was an offence committed in the case in which the different price terms offered to cash customers and to other customers were not made clear? Contrast *Read Bros Cycles (Leyton) Ltd* v *Waltham Forest London Borough Council* [1978] Crim LR 501 with *Barnes* v *Watts Tyre & Rubber Co. Ltd* [1978] RTR 405.

(b)   Was it unlawful actually to charge a price different to that advertised? This was assumed to be so in a number of cases, notably *J. Sainsbury Ltd* v *West Midlands County Council* (1982) 89 ITSA Monthly Review 211, but in *Miller* v *F. A. Sadd & Son Ltd* [1981] 3 All ER 265 and *Simmons* v *Emmett* [1982] TL 189 the Divisional Court ruled that a mistake in billing did not constitute an offence, for the reason that the advertised price was the correct price.

13.2.4   Other deficiencies and suggestions for reform

It may be seen from the above that the operation of s. 11 of the Trade Descriptions Act 1968 was far from satisfactory. Coupled with these specific problems were the general weaknesses that s. 11 applied only to goods and did not extend to services, accommodation or facilities, and that it was permissible for traders to use disclaimers of liability in the form of warnings that price comparisons and the like were not necessarily to be taken as conforming with the Trade Descriptions Act's requirements for validity.

The operation of s. 11 was given detailed consideration by the Director General of Fair Trading in a report published in 1976 (Cmnd 6628). The report expressed some reservation about the adoption of a general offence of misleading pricing, and instead suggested a number of amendments to s. 11 designed to overcome the problems of disclaimers, comparisons with previous prices, and 'value' and similar abstract claims. The extension of s. 11 to services, accommodation and facilities, and to hire and hire-purchase agreements, was also proposed. A direct consequence of the 1976 review was the introduction of the Price Marking (Bargain Offers) Order 1979, made under s. 4 of the Prices Act 1974.

13.3   Price Marking (Bargain Offers) Order 1979

13.3.1   Bargain offers

The Price Marking (Bargain Offers) Order 1979 (SI 1979 No. 364) applied to goods and services supplied to the public, and outlawed two forms of bargain offers, whether or not the facts stated in those offers were true (subject to an exemption in favour of commercial publishers and compilers of reports):

(a)   Claims to the effect that the price was lower than the value of the subject-matter.

(b)   Comparisons with the prices charged by any person in respect of the subject-matter in question, whether or not that other price is stated. This was, however, subject to a number of (almost incomprehensible) exceptions almost as wide as the prohibition itself. Thus, the courts ultimately decided that the phrase 'bargain price' did not infringe the Order while the phrase 'clearance offer' did amount to an offence (*West Yorkshire Metropolitan County Council* v *MFI Furniture Centre Ltd* [1983] 3 All ER 234) and that where a sale price is advertised no offence is committed if the original price is not also displayed (*Comet Radiovision Services Ltd* v *Williamson* [1983] 1 WLR 766).

13.3.2   Comparisons with recommended prices

The Order did not impose any general prohibition on comparisons by a retailer with the recommended prices of any person. However, it was recognised that recommended prices relating to certain classes of consumer goods bore little relationship to actual selling prices, and the Order therefore prohibited comparisons with recommended prices issued for those goods.

The most important goods affected were as follows:

(a)   Beds, including camp-beds, mattresses and headboards.

(b)   Powered domestic appliances, including dishwashers, washing machines, refrigerators and freezers, food processors, cookers etc., kettles, cooking utensils, coffee makers, food-warming devices, shavers, toothbrushes, appliances for drying and styling hair, blankets and portable space heaters.

(c)   Consumer electronic goods, including televisions and radios, tape recorders, video cassette recorders and hi-fi equipment.

(d) Carpets, including mats, rugs, carpet tiles and underlay.

(e) Furniture, including kitchen furniture and excluding only garden furniture and soft furnishings.

13.3.3 Proposals for reform

In 1981 the Director General of Fair Trading published a detailed review of the Order. His main conclusions were that its complexity had led to much misunderstanding of its provisions, that the uncertainty had rendered the Order almost unenforceable, that legitimate trading practices had possibly been outlawed and that the provisions of the Order should be tightened to enable it to achieve its ends. Notes for guidance issued by the Department of Trade and Industry did little to remove doubts as to the meaning of the Order.

13.4   Moves Towards a General Offence

Thorough analysis of the combined effects of s. 11 of the Trade Descriptions Act 1968 and the Price Marking (Bargain Offers) Order 1979 was undertaken by an inter-departmental committee, which reported in 1984. The report, which was for the most part unanimous, made a number of important recommendations:

(a) Both provisions should be replaced with a general offence of misleading pricing.

(b) A code of practice should be introduced containing, *inter alia*, practical guidance for traders.

(c) Specific rules should be introduced to regulate bargain offers (suggestions were contained in the report).

These views form the basis of Part III of the Consumer Protection Act 1987: a general offence of giving a misleading price indication has s. 20(1) been implemented, in the place of s. 11 and the Price Marking (Bargain Offers) Order 1979; this is to be supplemented by a code of practice; and regulations are to be made in order to implement, s. 25 among other things, detailed rules about the making of bargain s. 26 offers. It has been indicated by the government that the regulations will preserve the prohibitions on comparing prices with recommended prices in relation to the classes of goods set out in 13.3.2.

Chapter 14

Misleading Pricing

s. 20(1)   It is an offence for any person in the course of a business of his to give a misleading indication to any consumers as to the price at which any goods, services, accommodation or facilities are available. The elements of the offence, and available defences, will be considered in this chapter.

14.1   Persons Liable

s. 20(1)
s. 46(5)

s. 20(3)(b)
s. 20(3)(a)

s. 24(3)

Liability attaches to any person who gives a misleading price indication 'in the course of any business of his'. The concept of acting in the course of a business is discussed in 16.2. Liability is not confined to persons from whom goods, services, accommodation or facilities may be obtained, but extends to a person who is not in the business of supplying a subject-matter of the type in question and a person who gives the indication on behalf of another. Consequently, liability can attach to a variety of persons, ranging from a person who does not supply directly to the public to a commercial publisher whose business consists of publishing advertisements for distribution by suppliers, although in the latter case the Act provides a special defence.

14.2   Consumers

s. 20(6)
s. 20(6)(a)

s. 20(6)(b)

s. 20(6)(c)

The definition of 'consumer' varies according to the subject-matter to be supplied. In the case of goods a consumer is any person who might wish to be supplied for his own private use or consumption; in the case of services or facilities a consumer is any person who might wish to be supplied otherwise than for the purpose of any business of his; and in the case of accommodation a consumer is any person who might wish to go into occupation otherwise than for the purpose of any business of his. The drafting of the Act is curious in that goods must be for private use whereas services, accommodation and facilities must be for non-commercial use; it is nevertheless doubtful whether the difference in drafting has any significance.

The phrase 'might wish', common to each of the three definitions, s. 20(6)
carries the implication that an offence may be committed where the
subject-matter is merely capable of being put to private use. Thus the
fact that the phrase used is not 'might reasonably wish' seems to
confirm that the only subject-matter clearly outside this part of the
Act is one which no person could ever conceivably want to put to
private use.

14.3 Subject-Matter

14.3.1 Availability
The offence is committed by a misleading indication as to the price at
which the relevant subject-matter is 'available'. This formulation
doubtless catches all forms of advertising and display, but there s. 20(1)
would seem to be at least two situations—both of which caused
problems under the old law—to which it does not apply. First, there is
the practice of retailers advertising particular goods at discount
prices in order to tempt customers on to their premises, when in fact
those goods are not stocked at all or are stocked in limited quantities.
Here the misleading statement relates not to pricing but to
availability. Secondly, it will be recalled from chapter 13 that in *Miller
v F. A. Sadd & Son Ltd* [1981] 3 All ER 265 the court held that s. 11(2)
of the Trade Descriptions Act 1968 did not extend to the act of
charging a price different to that quoted. The position is apparently
no different under the 1987 Act: it is difficult to see how an incorrect
invoice is misleading as to the price at which goods are 'available'.

14.3.2 Goods
There are no restrictions on the general definition of 'goods' in this
part of the Act. The word thus encompasses substances, growing s. 45(1)
crops, things attached to land, ships, aircraft and vehicles. Goods
attached to land are caught whether or not their supply is to form a
part of the same contract under which an interest in land is to be
transferred.

14.3.3 Services and facilities
The terms 'services' and 'facilities' are not given exhaustive
definitions under the Act, but are stated to include:

(a) the provision of credit, banking or insurance services;   s. 22(1)(a)
(b) the purchase and sale of foreign currency;   s. 22(1)(b)
(c) the supply of electricity;   s. 22(1)(c)
(d) the provision of off-road parking facilities;   s. 22(1)(d)
(e) the provision of facilities for parking caravans (other than in s. 22(1)(e)
relation to occupation as a sole or main residence);

s. 23(2)(b)   (f)   the provision of services in relation to the creation or disposal of an interest in land, e.g., the services of a solicitor, surveyor or estate agent.

s. 22(2)   Services supplied under a contract of employment are excluded, as
s. 22(3)   are services or facilities provided in the course of an investment business by a person authorised to carry out that business by or under the Financial Services Act 1986.

14.3.4   Accommodation and facilities
s. 23   The offence of misleading pricing applies to a statement advertising the availability of an interest in land. The scope of the offence is nevertheless limited in a number of crucial respects:

s. 23(1)(a)   (a)   The person creating or disposing of the interest in land must do so in the course of a business.
s. 23(1)(b)   (b)   The misleading indication must relate to the creation or disposal of an interest in a 'new dwelling'. This is a building or any
s. 23(3)   part of a building (including outhouses etc.) which has been constructed or adapted to be occupied as a residence and which has not previously been occupied as a residence in its present form. The definition thus encompasses entirely new houses or flats, and commercial buildings converted into dwellings. The Act also specifically provides for the case in which a dwelling is converted into a series of smaller dwellings: each of those smaller dwellings is deemed to be a new dwelling in its own right despite the fact that the original building had been occupied previously as a dwelling.
s. 23(3)   (c)   The interest to be transferred must be either the freehold estate or a leasehold interest for not less than 21 years. The exclusion of short-term lets has been justified by the fact that such agreements are governed by the Rent Acts, although it is difficult to see why the application of those Acts should affect the prohibition on misleading pricing.
s. 23(1)(b)   (d)   The person acquiring the interest must do so in order to occupy the dwelling as a residence. This extends to sole, primary and secondary residences and, as the result of an amendment to the Bill in the House of Lords, residences purchased for future occupation.

It follows from the above factors that the Act is concerned only with the *first* disposal of a long-term interest in land to a consumer by a builder, developer or other commercial owner. The only exception to this principle arises where a building previously used as a dwelling is converted by a person acting in the course of a business into smaller dwellings. When the Act does apply, potential liability attaches to the person disposing of the interest as well as to any person acting on his behalf, such as an estate agent.

The primary concern of the draftsman here was with the plethora of special discounts, free appliances and the like which frequently accompany the sale of newly built dwellings. Such offers are now specifically controlled.

14.4   Prices

The 'price' of any goods, services, accommodation or facilities refers s. 20(6) to the aggregate (or method of calculating the aggregate) of the sums required to be paid by the consumer. Thus an offence may be committed if ancillary charges, such as VAT or mandatory insurance, are excluded in a misleading manner from a stated price.

One interesting question arising under the Act is its application to quotations and estimates for supply. A quotation is an unconditional offer which is capable of acceptance. If the supplier charges a price different to that in the quotation he will not be guilty of an offence if the discrepancy arises due to an error in the final billing, although he may face liability if the quotation itself had been misleadingly presented and the invoice was in accordance with the method of calculation actually used (see 14.3.1). An estimate, by contrast, is not an unconditional offer and is thus not capable of acceptance as such. However, there is nothing in the Act to prevent an offence being committed where a misleading estimate is prepared, despite the fact that the estimate itself is not without more intended to be a contractual document.

14.5   Misleading

14.5.1   General definition

A price indication may, for the purposes of the 1987 Act, be misleading in one of three senses: it may be misleading at the time at s. 21(1) which it is given; it may have become misleading as the result of s. 20(2) subsequent events; or, where no fixed price is involved, the method of s. 21(2) determining the price may be stated in a misleading fashion. In all cases the test of whether a price indication is misleading is based upon what the consumers to whom it was addressed might reasonably s. 21(1) infer. It is immaterial whether the indication is misleading to all s. 20(3)(c) consumers, or only to some of them.

14.5.2   Presently misleading price indications

A price indication is misleading if a consumer might reasonably infer any of the following matters:

s. 21(1)(a)   (a) The price is less than in fact it is.

s. 21(1)(b)   (b) The price is unconditional when in fact the price depends upon one or more conditions, e.g., purchase by a given date, in given quantities or in conjunction with some other subject-matter.

s. 21(1)(c)   (c) The price is fully inclusive, in that there are no additional charges, when in fact further charges are required. This clearly affects mandatory charges, such as VAT, and it might well be the case that an offence is committed where the price of so-called 'optional extras', which are in reality essential to the utility of the subject-matter, is not included in the price of the subject-matter itself.

s. 21(1)(d)   (d) The price is to be increased or reduced (whether or not at a specified time or by a specified amount) or maintained at its present or some future level, when the person giving the indication has no expectation that the price is to be altered or maintained. This catches assurances to customers to buy now as the price is shortly to go up, or encouragement given by a seller, who knows that the price is shortly to drop, to a consumer to buy now. Some difficulty has been anticipated in applying this provision to services in relation to the sale and purchase of foreign currency, given the inherent instability of currency markets and the difficulty of keeping fully abreast of the most recent rates.

s. 21(1)(e)   (e) Where the price advertised is compared either to some other price, to the value of the subject-matter or to the price or value of any other subject-matter, and the facts upon which the comparison is based are not as stated. This provision is concerned with outlawing false or misleading comparisons with, for example, prices charged by other traders or even with the quality of competing subject-matter available at a different price.

14.5.3   Price indications which become misleading

Where a price indication, which was correct at the time it was given, has become misleading due to the operation of subsequent events, the

s. 21(2)(a)   person giving the indication commits an offence if two conditions are satisfied:

s. 21(2)(b)   (a) it could reasonably be expected that consumers to whom the indication was originally given might rely upon it after it has become misleading; and

s. 21(2)(c)   (b) the person giving the indication has failed to take all reasonable steps to prevent reliance by those consumers.

What is reasonable will depend upon the nature of the original indication. If it was given to the public at large, there is probably little that can be done other than for an updated indication to be issued. By contrast, if the indication was given to specific persons who are easily traced, an updating of the position might reasonably be required to be given to each of them.

14.5.4 Misleading indications as to method of determining a price

The definition of a misleading indication of the method of determining a price closely follows the format set out in 14.5.3 for s. 21(2) misleading price indications. An indication is misleading as to a method of determining a price if a consumer might infer from the indication any of the following matters:

(a)   The method is not what it in fact is. s. 21(2)(a)

(b)   The method is unconditional when in fact it rests upon other s. 21(2)(b) facts or circumstances.

(c)   The method will produce a fully inclusive price when in fact s. 21(2)(c) further charges are to be imposed.

(d)   The method is to be changed or maintained when in fact the s. 21(2)(d) person giving the indication has no such expectation.

(e)   Where the method advertised is compared to some other s. 21(2)(e) method, that the comparison is based upon facts or circumstances other than those on which it is in fact based.

14.5.5   Corrections and disclaimers

An issue which has bedevilled the operation of the Trade Descriptions Act 1968 is the extent to which a false statement can be nullified by suitable words of correction or disclaimer. There was little authority on this matter under s. 11 of that Act, although in *Doble* v *David Greig Ltd* [1972] 2 All ER 195 the Divisional Court indicated that a false price indication was capable of correction by a properly worded notice placed in close proximity to the goods bearing the false indication. The validity of disclaimers as to the accuracy of prices was uncertain, although most retailers operated on the assumption that it was legitimate to side-step possible breaches of s. 11 of the Trade Descriptions Act 1968 by general words of disclaimer. The position under the Price Marking (Bargain Offers) Order 1979 was equally unclear.

The 1987 Act does not mention corrections or disclaimers, but it is probable that they will be pressed into use by traders. It is suggested that it ought to be legitimate for a trader to be able to correct a misleading impression by suitable wording: thus, where a product mistakenly bears two different prices, a prominent notice near to the product indicating one or other of those prices ought to be regarded as correcting any misunderstanding and thus preventing an offence from being committed in the first place. However, it is difficult to see why the law should confer any further protection in favour of a possible offender. By way of example, a notice attached to a quotation indicating that the supplier accepts no responsibility for any inaccuracy in the quotation might well have some effect in civil law, but it is unlikely to nullify a charge that the quotation was

s. 26(3)(e)   misleading. The question of disclaimers may, however, be resolved by regulations which the Secretary of State is empowered to make under this Part of the Act: this power is discussed in 15.2.

14.6   Defences

A number of defences are available to a charge of giving a misleading price indication and to a charge of giving a price indication which has become misleading. These defences range from the general to the

s. 25   specific, and in all cases the provisions of the code of practice, to be issued under the Act, may be taken into account.

s. 39   (a)   The accused has a defence to a charge of giving a misleading price indication if he can show that he took all reasonable steps and exercised all due diligence to avoid committing the offence. The

s. 20(2)(c)   defence is not available to a charge of failing to correct a price indication which has become misleading, as an element of that offence is the failure of the accused to take reasonable precautions. Due diligence is discussed in 16.3.

s. 24(1)   (b)   It is a defence for the accused to prove that his acts or omissions were authorised by regulations made by the Secretary of

s. 26(1)   State under Part III of the Act: for discussion of the power to make regulations, see 15.2.

s. 24(2)   (c)   Where a misleading price indication is contained in a book, newspaper, magazine, film or broadcast, it is a defence for the accused to show that the indication was not contained in any advertisement. A person who is not seeking to promote a product but who is merely providing information about it is thus protected.

s. 24(3)   (d)   A person whose business is publishing or arranging for the
s. 24(3)(a)   publishing of advertisements, and who publishes a misleading price
s. 24(3)(b)   indication based on information provided to him, has a defence if he can demonstrate that he received the information in the ordinary
s. 24(3)(c)   course of business and that, at the time of publication, he neither knew nor had grounds for suspecting that publication would involve the commission of an offence. This defence is also available where the charge is failure to correct a price indication which has become misleading.

s. 24(4)   (e)   A specific defence is provided for a supplier (whether producer or wholesaler) who recommends a reselling price to his

customers and who advertises the recommended price to consumers
in the belief that it was being followed. The formal elements of the
defence are: the supplier did not himself supply the subject-matter to   s. 24(4)(a)
consumers; a resale price had been recommended to all dealers; the   s. 24(4)(b)
price indication as advertised to consumers was misleading only by   s. 24(4)(c)
reason of one or more dealers failing to adopt the recommendation;
and it was reasonable for the supplier to assume that the   s. 24(4)(d)
recommendation was for the most part being followed. Two points
should here be borne in mind. First, the *imposition* of minimum resale
prices is unlawful under the Resale Prices Act 1976. Secondly, the
Price Marking (Bargain Offers) Order 1979, which is to be repealed
under the 1987 Act and to be replaced by regulations with a like   s. 26
effect, prohibits, in relation to a wide range of household goods,
comparisons of retail prices with recommended resale prices.

Chapter 15

Guidance, Additional Powers and Enforcement

15.1 Code of Practice on Pricing

15.1.1 Status of the Price Code

The original version of the Consumer Protection Bill introduced into the House of Lords made provision for the issue of a Price Code by the Secretary of State, following consultation with the Director General of Fair Trading and such other persons as the Secretary of State considered appropriate. The code was to have two purposes. First, it was intended to provide general guidance to traders on their pricing procedures. Secondly, it was to play a substantial, but not for all purposes conclusive, part in establishing whether the offence of giving a misleading pricing indication had been committed. In its latter role the code was significant in two respects: any contravention of the code was to be taken into account by the court in determining whether an offence had been committed; and compliance with the code was to be an absolute defence to a charge of giving a misleading price indication.

The Price Code in this form ran into severe difficulties in the House of Lords on two grounds. First, many of their lordships regarded the concept of a code, which purported to proffer advice to traders and at the same time to act both as an absolute defence and as an aid to prosecution, as inappropriate. In their view the advisory and evidential functions were entirely different and ought not to have been combined in one document. Secondly, their lordships raised the important constitutional point that the Bill provided for a code which did not require parliamentary approval but which was nevertheless relevant to criminal charges: it was unacceptable to the Upper House that a document with such significance and which provided a gloss on primary legislation would not be capable of parliamentary scrutiny.

As soon as it was faced with these objections, and while the Bill was still being debated in the Upper House, the government took the unusual steps of (a) issuing a consultative document requesting opinions on the proper form and content of a code, (b) agreeing to drop from the Bill those provisions which gave the code a status more than that of guidance to traders and of reserving the right to reinstate the code in something approaching its original form in the House of Commons as the result of its consultations. In the event the consultation process produced a strong reaction against a multipurpose code. The government, faced with this fact and the further fact that as a result of the dissolution of Parliament the Bill had just a few days to complete its passage, decided not to reverse the decisions reached in the House of Lords.

The relevant features of the Price Code are these:

(a) The code is to be issued by the Secretary of State following s. 25(1) consultations with the Director General of Fair Trading and such other persons as the Secretary of State considers appropriate.

(b) The code is to be made in the form of a statutory instrument s. 25(4) and thus open to parliamentary scrutiny should any member of either House choose to challenge any part of it.

(c) The code will provide practical guidance with respect to the s. 25(1)(a) requirements of the offence of giving a misleading price indication.

(d) The code will promote what appear to the Secretary of State s. 25(1)(b) to be desirable practices with respect to giving price indications.

(e) Contravention of the code is not of itself to give rise to any s. 21(2) civil or criminal liability. However, any such contravention may be relied upon by the prosecutor in establishing that the accused s. 21(2)(a) committed the offence or in negativing any defence open to the accused.

(f) The accused may rely on the code for the purpose of s. 21(2)(b) establishing either that he did not commit an offence or that he had a defence.

It is to be stressed that the code, for the purposes of (e) and (f) s. 21(2) above, is not conclusive evidence of anything.

15.1.2 Contents of the Price Code

Discussions about the structure and content of the code were taking place during the passage through Parliament of the Consumer Protection Bill, the third and most recent draft of the code having been issued in November 1986. However, following the change in the status of the code from that originally anticipated by the government, it has been admitted by the government that major revisions will be required, principally to remove mandatory rules and to replace them with more general guidance on what is misleading and what is desirable.

For these reasons the November 1986 draft of the Price Code would now appear to be of little real significance, and has not been

appended to this book. However, the new code to be introduced
under the Act might be expected to deal with the following issues
which were covered in the draft:

(a)   comparisons by a trader with his own past prices;

(b)   duration of introductory offers;

(c)   comparisons by a trader with the prices of his competitors;

(d)   comparisons between similar goods in different conditions,
e.g., 'seconds', 'ready assembled', etc;

(e)   comparisons with manufacturers' recommended prices (to
the extent that such comparisons will be permitted by regulations re-
enacting the prohibitions established under the Price Marking
(Bargain Offers) Order 1979);

(f)   'value' and 'worth' claims;

(g)   seasonal and other 'sales';

(h)   free offers;

(i)   principles governing the display by a trader of different prices
for the same product;

(j)   failure to include all charges in the stated price.

It may be anticipated from this list, and from the report of the inter-
departmental committee in 1984, referred to in 13.3, that most of the
guidance will be confined to the area of bargain offers, previously
covered by the 1979 Order. The code is certain to set out reasonably
firm guidelines on which forms of bargain offers are misleading and
which are innocuous. The legal rules concerning bargain offers will be
s. 26   contained in regulations to be made under Part III of the Act.

15.2   Supplementary Regulations

s. 26(1)   The Act confers upon the Secretary of State the power to make
s. 26(1)(a)   regulations dealing with the circumstances and manner in which price
s. 26(1)(b)   indications are given and facilitating the enforcement of the
              misleading price indications provisions. Regulations are to be
s. 26(2)(a)   applicable only to price indications given in the course of a business.
s. 26(2)(b)   This principle is, however, subject to an exception—inserted by the
              House of Lords—relating to goods or services supplied by a landlord
              or licensor of premises. The purpose behind this amendment is to
              permit the government to introduce regulations prohibiting
              misleading price indications as to the original and resale prices of gas
              and electricity supplied to tenants and licensees. The government has
              indeed stated its intention to introduce regulations on this point as
              soon as the Act comes into force.

The scope of regulations is not restricted and they may govern both substantive and procedural issues. As far as substantive issues are concerned, regulations may, *inter alia*:

(a)   prohibit a price indication from referring to specified matters (a provision which will be used to establish new rules for bargain offers);   s. 26(3)(a)

(b)   require a price indication to be accompanied by an explanation or other additional information;   s. 26(3)(b)

(c)   require explanations or additional information to be accurate;   s. 26(3)(d)

(d)   prohibit or restrict disclaimers;   s. 26(3)(e)

(e)   establish presumptions about the meaning of words used in price indications (e.g., to take an example from the repealed s. 11 of the Trade Descriptions Act 1968, that the term 'recommended price' is to be presumed to be referring to the manufacturer's recommended price unless the trader indicates to the contrary).   s. 26(3)(f)

Procedurally, regulations may require the provision of accurate explanations or additional information to officers of enforcement authorities and provide for any contravention of the regulations to be a criminal offence.   s. 26(3) (c), (d)   s. 26(3) (g), (h)

15.3   Enforcement

The enforcement of Part III of the Consumer Protection Act 1987 follows, with only necessary modifications, the principles discussed in chapter 11 established for the enforcement of safety provisions. The following discussion summarises the main enforcement provisions applicable to pricing offences: the reader is referred to chapter 11 for more detailed analysis.

15.3.1   Enforcement authorities
Enforcement of the pricing provisions, i.e., the offences of giving a misleading price indication and of contravening any regulations made under Part III, is carried out by local weights and measures authorities. This had been the position under s. 11 of the Trade Descriptions Act 1968 and under the Price Marking (Bargain Offers) Order 1979. The costs of enforcement are borne by the enforcement authority, although where a person has been successfully prosecuted under the pricing provisions he may be ordered by the court to reimburse the authority for costs incurred by it in seizing and detaining goods.   s. 27(1)   s. 35

15.3.2   Test purchases

s. 28(1)   An enforcement authority is empowered to make a test purchase of
            any goods, services, accommodation or facilities. If the test leads to
s. 28(2)   the bringing of criminal proceedings, the person from whom the
            subject-matter was obtained, and any other person interested in it, is
            entitled to a retest, in so far as that is practicable.

15.3.3   Obtaining evidence and information

s. 29   Officers of enforcement authorities may examine documents and
s. 29(1)   goods to determine whether offences against the pricing provisions
s. 29(2)   have been committed. To this end they are empowered at any
            reasonable hour to enter premises, inspect goods and require the
s. 29(5)   production of business records. Goods and records may be seized and
            detained by an officer if he has reasonable grounds for believing that
            they may be required in evidence in criminal proceedings under Part
            III.

                If entry to premises cannot be effected, an officer may obtain a
s. 30(2)(a) warrant from a magistrate if there are reasonable grounds for
            believing that goods or records on the premises provide evidence of a
            pricing offence or that an offence has taken, or is about to take, place
s. 30(2)(b) on those premises. A warrant may be issued only where the
            magistrate is satisfied that the officer would not otherwise gain entry
            or that without a warrant the evidence might disappear.

s. 32   There are a number of offences established dealing with the
s. 32(1)(a) obstruction of an enforcement officer. These include: obstruction;
s. 32(1)(b) failure to comply with a valid requirement imposed by an officer;
s. 32(1)(c) failing to provide reasonable assistance or information; and
s. 32(2)   knowingly or recklessly making a material false statement.

15.3.4   Seizure and detention of goods

            Goods may be seized by an enforcement officer on two grounds only:

s. 29(5)(b) (a)   to determine whether an offence has been committed;
s. 29(6)(a) (b)   for use as evidence in criminal proceedings.

s. 33(1),   Any person interested in the goods may thereafter apply to a
(2)   magistrates' court for an order for their release. An order for release
s. 33(3)   will be made if the court is satisfied that the goods have been detained
            for six months without proceedings having been brought.

s. 34   Where goods have been detained, and it later proves to be the case
            that no pricing offence had been committed, the enforcement
            authority is liable to pay compensation to any person with an interest
            in the goods. Compensation is not, apparently, available where a
            prosecution is not commenced within the six-month period allowed
            for detention.

15.3.5 Proceedings

Criminal proceedings may be brought only by enforcement s. 27(1)
authorities. Civil proceedings do not lie under the Act for the s. 41(2)
infringement of any pricing provision and contracts are not, subject s. 41(3)
to their own terms, to be affected by such an infringement. It may well
be the case, however, that the giving of a misleading price indication
will amount to at least misrepresentation, if not full breach of
contract.

Chapter 16

Supplementary and Miscellaneous Provisions

16.1 'Supply'

16.1.1 General definition of 'supply'

The concept of 'supply' is crucial to the entire Consumer Protection Act 1987. Early consumer protection legislation, notably the Consumer Protection Act 1961, conferred upon this term a limited meaning, and the definition adopted in the 1987 Act—re-enacted from the Consumer Safety Act 1978—seeks to catch every manner in

s. 46   which goods may be provided to a consumer by a trader. Supply may take any of the following forms:

s. 46(1)(a)   (a) selling, hiring or lending out goods (in the case of hiring or
s. 46(8)   lending out, renewal of the agreement is deemed not to be a fresh supply);

s. 46(1)(b)   (b) entering into a hire-purchase agreement (subsequent exercise by the hirer of the option to purchase is deemed not to be a fresh supply) or a contract for work and materials;

s. 46(1)(c)   (c) the performance of a contract for work and materials;
s. 46(1)(d)   (d) providing the goods in exchange for any consideration (including trading stamps) other than money;

s. 46(1)(e)   (e) providing the goods in or in connection with the performance of any statutory function;

s. 46(1)(f)   (f) giving the goods as a prize or gift.

16.1.2 Supply of goods on credit

The supply of expensive consumer goods commonly involves the provision of credit by a person other than the dealer. In the typical hire-purchase, conditional sale or hiring agreement, the dealer does not himself supply the goods to the consumer but supplies them to the creditor who in turn lets or sells them to the consumer, retaining title in the goods as security. It will be seen that, as a matter of law, there is no contract of supply between dealer and consumer, but the Act

s. 46(2)   nevertheless treats the dealer, rather than the person providing finance, as the supplier. The justification of this is that, as a matter of commercial reality, the legal supplier does not make representations to the consumer as to the price of the goods, nor does he have a realistic opportunity to test their safety.

16.1.3   Supply of goods comprised in land

The Act here draws a number of distinctions. First, in the comparatively rare case in which goods comprised in land are supplied to a consumer unaccompanied by a transfer of any interest in the land itself, e.g., where fixtures and fittings are sold, the goods are fully within the Act. Secondly, the transfer of a building by way of sale or lease by a person acting in the course of a business is outside s. 46(4) the Act for all purposes other than its misleading pricing provisions and notices to warn under Part II of the Act; a building cannot be the subject of an action under the product liability provisions of Part I nor is it affected by the remaining provisions of Part II. Thirdly, s. 46(3) goods which are the constituent parts of buildings are deemed to be supplied by the builder as goods in their own right: such goods are within the product liability and misleading pricing provisions of the Act, but are outside its consumer safety provisons other than in relation to notices to warn.

16.1.4   Goods supplied as scrap

Goods which are supplied for the value of their constituent materials, s. 46(7)(b) as opposed to supply for their value as goods, fall outside the safety and misleading pricing provisions of the Act. However, prohibition notices and suspension notices continue to be available in relation to goods supplied as scrap.

16.2   Supply in the Course of a Business

16.2.1   Supply ancillary to a main business

The offences involving supply in Parts II and III of the Act all require the supplier to be acting 'in the course of a business of his . . . but it shall be immaterial whether the business is a business of dealing in the s. 46(5) goods'. This formulation is rather different from that found in other consumer protection legislation—it is more common to find words such as 'in the course of a trade or business' (see the Trade Descriptions Act 1968, s. 1, and the Sale of Goods Act 1979, s. 14). Authorities on the latter formulation indicate that there is a sale in the course of a business where selling is an integral part of the business (even though the business is not primarily that of dealing in goods), whereas isolated sales by a person in business fall outside the wording. Thus in *Havering London Borough Council v Stevenson* [1970] 3 All ER 609 it was held that a car-hire firm, which habitually sold off its cars once they had outlived their usefulness, was selling in the course of its business, but by contrast, in *Davies* v *Sumner* [1984] 3 All ER 831 the House of Lords decided that a travelling salesman who had sold his car had not done so in the course of a business as the car had been a mere adjunct and not part of any stock-in-trade.

The important question in the context of the Consumer Protection Act 1987 is whether the addition of the words 'but it shall be immaterial whether the business is a business of dealing in the goods' is significant. It is thought that they merely codify the above decisions: *Davies* v *Sumner* is unaffected if for no other reason than that the sale there was not in the course of any business; and the court in *Havering London Borough Council* v *Stevenson* was clear that there could be a sale in the course of a business even if that business was not selling.

16.2.2   Supply as a hobby

Where a person supplies goods in his spare time and as a hobby, it may be a nice question whether he is nevertheless acting in the course of a business. In the leading authority, *Blakemore* v *Bellamy* [1983] RTR 303, a postman, who in his spare time carried out repairs to old cars and resold them, was held not to have been acting in the course of a business; the Court of Appeal accepted that it was possible for a person to be acting in the course of a business by conducting a spare-time activity, but that the evidence did not establish that situation in the instant case. By contrast, writing poetry as a hobby has been held to be a business activity (*Eiman* v *London Borough of Waltham Forest* (1982) ITSA Monthly Review 204).

16.2.3   Supply of reconditioned goods

Blakemore v *Bellamy* [1983] RTR 303 demonstrates that, in principle, buying, reconditioning and reselling goods of a similar description can amount to the business of supplying goods of that description. However, a business of that nature is deemed to fall outside Parts II

s. 46(7)(a)   and III of the Consumer Protection Act 1987 for all purposes other than in connection with prohibition notices and suspension notices.

16.3   'Due Diligence' Defence

16.3.1   Availability and scope of the defence

The specific defences to prosecutions provided by the Consumer Protection Act 1987 are supplemented by the general defence that the

s. 39(1)   person charged 'took all reasonable steps and exercised all due

s. 39(5)   diligence' to avoid committing the offence. The defence is available to the following charges:

(a)   infringing the general safety requirement by supply etc. (s. 10(1));

(b)   infringing any safety regulations by supply etc. (s. 12(1));

(c)   failing to test goods in accordance with safety regulations (s. 12(2));

(d)   failing to attach a mark or other information to goods in accordance with safety regulations (s. 12(3));

(e)   contravening a suspension notice (s. 14(6));

(f)   giving a misleading price indication (s. 20(1)).

The defence is a familiar one in consumer protection legislation, and similar wording is to be found in weights and measures, food and drugs, trade descriptions and consumer credit legislation. However, the ambit of the defence in the 1987 Act is somewhat wider than some of its counterparts, which additionally require the defendant to prove that the offence arose from one or more specified causes, for example, that the accused acted under a mistake, that he relied upon information supplied to him by another or that the offence was due to the act or default of another. Such matters remain relevant under the 1987 Act, not as a prerequisite of the defence but as elements of the overall reasonableness of the accused's conduct.

Experience under other consumer protection legislation has demonstrated that reliance on information supplied by another and the act or default of another are the main grounds on which a defendant will seek to excuse himself. The 1987 Act contains two provisions to deal with pleas of this type. First, where the accused s. 39(4) asserts that he relied upon information supplied by another, in order to substantiate his defence he must show that it was reasonable for him to rely upon the information, having regard in particular to steps which were and might have been taken to verify it, and whether he had any reason to disbelieve the information. Secondly, where the s. 39(2), accused claims that the reason for the offence was either the act or (3) default of another or his reliance on information given by another, he must, at least seven days before the hearing, serve a notice on the prosecutor identifying the person upon whom the commission of the offence is blamed: if this does not happen, the accused cannot rely upon the defence. It must, however, be doubted whether these provisions are fully appropriate to the defence under the 1987 Act which, as noted above, does not specify the grounds on which a defence may be made out but rests merely on reasonable steps and due diligence: they seem to be directly applicable only to those statutes which state that the conduct of another person is a prerequisite to reliance upon the due diligence defence. Nevertheless, the effect of these provisions is that the accused will not be able to establish that he acted with due diligence by relying on information supplied by another unless he can show that his reliance was reasonable and unless that other is identified.

16.3.2   Practical application of the defence

As a matter of practice there have proved to be two classes of case in which the due diligence defence has been raised: where a company alleges that its crime was due to the misconduct of an employee; and where a supplier of goods claims that he relied upon information provided to him by the person from whom he obtained the goods.

16.3.2.1 Employment cases   The leading authority is *Tesco Supermarkets Ltd* v *Nattrass* [1972] AC 153, in which the House of Lords held that a company has a defence where the crime was the result of the act or default of an employee if two requirements are satisfied: (a) the employee in question is relatively junior, as a senior employee who participates in the management of the company's business is in essence the *alter ego* of the firm; (b) the company has taken all reasonable precautions in the training of its employees and has established adequate supervisory procedures. Failure to supervise, or to issue adequate instructions to, employees once a problem has emerged, will lead to the conclusion that the company has not acted with all due diligence in its attempts to prevent an offence from occurring: see *McNab* v *Alexanders* 1971 SLT 121, *Nattrass* v *Timpson Shops Ltd* [1973] Crim LR 197 and *Haringey London Borough Council* v *Piro Shoes Ltd* [1976] Crim LR 462.

16.3.2.2 Resale cases   Where a seller simply resells goods, acting in reliance on what he has been told by the person from whom he received supplies, the Act, codifying previous authorities, makes it clear that such reliance must have been reasonable. This means for the most part that the seller must take elementary precautions to check the accuracy of the information. To take some examples, a seller cannot claim to have acted with due diligence if:

(a)   he fails to check whether watches claimed to be waterproof can withstand temporary immersion (*Sherratt* v. *Geralds The American Jewellers Ltd* (1970) 114 SJ 147);

(b)   he does not test the paint on toy soldiers for possible lead content (*Taylor* v *Lawrence Fraser (Bristol) Ltd* (1977) 121 SJ 757);

(c)   he makes no attempt to inquire into the past history of a car but relies upon the assurances of the seller or the odometer reading (*Zawadski* v *Sleigh* [1975] RTR 113; *Barker* v *Hargreaves* (1981) 125 SJ 165; *Simmons* v *Potter* [1975] RTR 347; *Wandsworth London Borough Council* v *Bentley* [1980] RTR 429; *Crook* v *Howells Garages (Newport) Ltd* [1980] RTR 434).

16.4   Liability of Other Persons

16.4.1   Liability of employees

It was seen in 16.3.2.1 that the main effect of *Tesco Supermarkets Ltd v Nattrass* [1972] AC 153 is in some circumstances to relieve a company from criminal liability where the offence is due to the act or default of a junior, but not a senior, employee. A consequence of this is that a defaulting junior employee may be prosecuted in his private capacity (although this will rarely be justified and in practice rarely happens) whereas in the case of a defaulting senior employee the company itself and not the employee faces liability.

The position in law would appear to be the very reverse of what it ought to be, and the 1987 Act makes provision for the prosecution of senior employees. Where a company is guilty of an offence as a result s. 40(2) of the consent, connivance or neglect of any director, manager, secretary or similar officer, that person as well as the company is deemed to be guilty of the offence. Liability extends to a person who s. 40(2) has not been appointed formally to any office, but who purports to act in an official capacity. In the case of a company managed by its s. 40(3) members—the small private company—the defaulting member faces liability in the same way. The word 'neglect' in this provision has been held to mean something more than failure to take all reasonable precautions: see *R* v *R. McMillan Aviation Ltd* [1981] Crim LR 785 and *Lewin* v *Bland* (1983) 148 JP 69.

16.4.2   Other persons liable

The Consumer Protection Act 1987 contains a cross-over liability provision common to other legislation in the field. This provides that s. 40(1) if A commits an offence due to the act or default of B, B himself is deemed to have committed that offence and may be prosecuted whether or not proceedings are taken against A. In many cases it will be unnecessary to rely on this indirect liability provision in order to prosecute B, as B may have committed a direct offence, under the Act, of supply etc. However, its use is necessary in two cases: to permit the prosecution of a person not otherwise facing liability under the Act, such as a person not acting in the course of any business of his (*Olgeirsson* v *Kitching* [1986] 1 All ER 746); and to enable an enforcement authority with jurisdiction over A's direct offence to prosecute B in indirect proceedings even though B's direct supply offence was committed outside its jurisdiction.

Indirect liability under the cross-over provision requires proof of two matters: that A has committed an offence under the Act; and that the offence was caused by the act or default of B.

16.4.2.1   The commission of an offence by A   Proof of A's offence will not in most cases give rise to any difficulty, particularly where there has been a previous successful prosecution of A. However, one serious practical problem could arise because of interaction between the due diligence defence available to A and the imposition of indirect liability on B. Suppose, for example, that B, by supplying an unsafe product to A coupled with assurances about its safety, causes A to commit an offence by resupplying that product. If A is prosecuted, A may well be able to demonstrate that he took all reasonable precautions and exercised all due diligence in his reliance on B's assurances and that he is entitled to be acquitted. A is thus not guilty, and for that reason B escapes indirect liability as B cannot be said to have caused A to commit an offence. Similarly, where A is not prosecuted, the drafting of the Act leaves it open to B to defend himself in cross-over proceedings by the curious pleading that A's reliance on him entitles him to be acquitted.

s. 39(1)
s. 40(1)

This problem has arisen in the context of the similarly worded Trade Descriptions Act 1968, and was resolved in *Tesco Supermarkets Ltd* v *Nattrass* [1972] AC 153 (applied in *Coupe* v *Guyett* [1973] 2 All ER 1058). The House of Lords here decided that a due diligence defence open to A based on his reliance on B is to be disregarded for the purposes of B's indirect liability. Consequently, B is entitled to be acquitted under the indirect liability provision only where A has a defence not based on his reliance on B.

16.4.2.2   Causation   There must be a causative link between B's act or omission and A's commission of the offence. A difficulty has here arisen under the Trade Descriptions Act 1968, for the courts have held, in a series of decisions culminating in *K. Lill Holdings Ltd* v *White* [1979] RTR 120, that the mere fact that goods have been supplied by B to A cannot be said to be the cause of any subsequent offence committed by A in supplying those goods, on the basis that what A does with the goods is outside B's control. This approach is artificial, particularly where A is a dealer in the goods and could have acquired them only for resale purposes, but it remains uncertain what further factors are necessary to forge the causative link where B has done no more than to supply goods to A.

16.5   Legislation Repealed

16.5.1   Trade Descriptions Act 1972
The Trade Descriptions Act 1972 sought to do away with certain forms of misleading indications of origin. It provided that where a

United Kingdom name or mark was applied to goods produced outside the United Kingdom, the supplier committed an offence by supplying those goods in the United Kingdom without a conspicuous indication of their country of origin. The Act did not apply to second-hand goods, and provided for the exemption of goods from its operation by statutory instrument: the main items excluded were foods blended from the produce of more than one country and drugs.

The Act was welcomed by United Kingdom consumers and manufacturers alike, but there had long been a recognition that the Act probably contravened art. 30 of the Treaty of Rome by imposing restrictions on imports which did not apply to goods produced at home. In 1986 the European Commission indicated that it would be taking formal infringement proceedings against the British government if the Act were not repealed, and the Consumer Protection Act 1987 has now taken that step. The government is s. 48(2)(a) understood to be examining ways of reintroducing the origin-marking requirement in a manner consistent with the Treaty of Rome, possibly along the lines of making it an offence under the Trade Descriptions Act 1968 for goods to carry the impression that they originate from some place other than their actual place of origin. An undertaking was given to Parliament during the passage of the Consumer Protection Bill that the repeal of the Trade Descriptions Act 1972 and the introduction of its replacement provision would be synchronised.

16.5.2 Fabrics (Misdescription) Act 1913
The Fabrics (Misdescription) Act 1913 made it a criminal offence for any person to sell, expose or have in his possession for sale any fabric—whether in the piece or made up into garments—which is marked or advertised as having any qualities of inflammability, unless the fabric conformed to standards established in regulations made by the Secretary of State. The Act was enforced by local weights and measures authorities. Specific safety regulations have, however, rendered the Act superfluous and the 1987 Act provides for its repeal. s. 48(2)(b)

Text of the Consumer Protection Act 1987

1987, c.43. An Act to make provision with respect to the liability of persons for damage caused by defective products; to consolidate with amendments the Consumer Safety Act 1978 and the Consumer Safety (Amendment) Act 1986; to make provision with respect to the giving of price indications; to amend Part I of the Health and Safety at Work etc. Act 1974 and sections 31 and 80 of the Explosives Act 1875; to repeal the Trade Descriptions Act 1972 and the Fabrics (Misdescription) Act 1913; and for connected purposes. [Royal assent 15 May 1987.]

B E IT ENACTED by the Queen's most Excellent Majesty, by and with the advice and consent of the Lords Spiritual and Temporal, and Commons, in this present Parliament assembled, and by the authority of the same, as follows:—

Part I   Product Liability

Purpose and construction of Part I
1.—(1)   This Part shall have effect for the purpose of making such provision as is necessary in order to comply with the product liability Directive and shall be construed accordingly.

   (2)   In this Part, except in so far as the context otherwise requires—

'agricultural produce' means any produce of the soil, of stock-farming or of fisheries;
   'dependent' and 'relative' have the same meaning as they have in, respectively, the Fatal Accidents Act 1976 and the Damages (Scotland) Act 1976;
   'producer', in relation to a product, means—

   (a) the person who manufactured it;
   (b) in the case of a substance which has not been manufactured but has been won or abstracted, the person who won or abstracted it;
   (c) in the case of a product which has not been manufactured, won or abstracted but essential characteristics of which are attributable to an industrial or other process having been carried out (for example, in relation to agricultural produce), the person who carried out that process;

'product' means any goods or electricity and (subject to subsection (3) below) includes a product which is comprised in another product, whether by virtue of being a component part or raw material or otherwise; and 'the product liability Directive' means the Directive of the Council of the European Communities, dated 25th July 1985, (No. 85/374/EEC) on the approximation of the laws, regulations and administrative provisions of the member States concerning liability for defective products.

(3)   For the purposes of this Part a person who supplies any product in which products are comprised, whether by virtue of being component parts or raw materials or otherwise, shall not be treated by reason only of his supply of that product as supplying any of the products so comprised.

Liability for defective products

2.—(1)   Subject to the following provisions of this Part, where any damage is caused wholly or partly by a defect in a product, every person to whom subsection (2) below applies shall be liable for the damage.

(2)   This subsection applies to—

(a)   the producer of the product;

(b)   any person who, by putting his name on the product or using a trade mark or other distinguishing mark in relation to the product, has held himself out to be the producer of the product;

(c)   any person who has imported the product into a member State from a place outside the member States in order, in the course of any business of his, to supply it to another.

(3)   Subject as aforesaid, where any damage is caused wholly or partly by a defect in a product, any person who supplied the product (whether to the person who suffered the damage, to the producer of any product in which the product in question is comprised or to any other person) shall be liable for the damage if—

(a)   the person who suffered the damage requests the supplier to identify one or more of the persons (whether still in existence or not) to whom subsection (2) above applies in relation to the product;

(b)   that request is made within a reasonable period after the damage occurs and at a time when it is not reasonably practicable for the person making the request to identify all those persons; and

(c)   the supplier fails, within a reasonable period after receiving the request, either to comply with the request or to identify the person who supplied the product to him.

(4)   Neither subsection (2) nor subsection (3) above shall apply to a person in respect of any defect in any game or agricultural produce if the only supply of the game or produce by that person to another was at a time when it had not undergone an industrial process.

(5)   Where two or more persons are liable by virtue of this Part for the same damage, their liability shall be joint and several.

(6)   This section shall be without prejudice to any liability arising otherwise than by virtue of this Part.

Meaning of 'defect'

3.—(1)   Subject to the following provisions of this section, there is a defect in a product for the purposes of this Part if the safety of the product is not such as persons generally are entitled to expect; and for those purposes 'safety', in relation to a product, shall include safety with respect to products comprised in that product and safety in the context of risks of damage to property, as well as in the context of risks of death or personal injury.

(2)   In determining for the purposes of subsection (1) above what persons generally are entitled to expect in relation to a product all the circumstances shall be taken into account, including—

(a)   the manner in which, and purposes for which, the product has been marketed, its get-up, the use of any mark in relation to the product and any instructions for, or warnings with respect to, doing or refraining from doing anything with or in relation to the product;

(b)   what might reasonably be expected to be done with or in relation to the product; and

(c)   the time when the product was supplied by its producer to another;

and nothing in this section shall require a defect to be inferred from the fact alone that the safety of a product which is supplied after that time is greater than the safety of the product in question.

Defences

4.—(1)   In any civil proceedings by virtue of this Part against any person ('the person proceeded against') in respect of a defect in a product it shall be a defence for him to show—

(a)   that the defect is attributable to compliance with any requirement imposed by or under any enactment or with any Community obligation; or

(b)   that the person proceeded against did not at any time supply the product to another; or

(c)   that the following conditions are satisfied, that is to say—

(i)   that the only supply of the product to another by the person proceeded against was otherwise than in the course of a business of that person's; and

(ii)   that section 2(2) above does not apply to that person or applies to him by virtue only of things done otherwise than with a view to profit; or

(d)   that the defect did not exist in the product at the relevant time; or

(e)   that the state of scientific and technical knowledge at the relevant time was not such that a producer of products of the same description as the product in question might be expected to have discovered the defect if it had existed in his products while they were under his control; or

(f)   that the defect—

(i)   constituted a defect in a product ('the subsequent product') in which the product in question had been comprised; and

(ii)   was wholly attributable to the design of the subsequent product or to compliance by the producer of the product in question with instructions given by the producer of the subsequent product.

(2)   In this section 'the relevant time', in relation to electricity, means the time at which it was generated, being a time before it was transmitted or distributed, and in relation to any other product, means—

(a)   if the person proceeded against is a person to whom subsection (2) of section 2 above applies in relation to the product, the time when he supplied the product to another;

(b)   if that subsection does not apply to that person in relation to the product, the time when the product was last supplied by a person to whom that subsection does apply in relation to the product.

Damage giving rise to liability
5.—(1)   Subject to the following provisions of this section, in this Part 'damage' means death or personal injury or any loss of or damage to any property (including land).

(2)   A person shall not be liable under section 2 above in respect of any defect in a product for the loss of or any damage to the product itself or for the loss of or any damage to the whole or any part of any product which has been supplied with the product in question comprised in it.

(3)   A person shall not be liable under section 2 above for any loss of or damage to any property which, at the time it is lost or damaged, is not—

(a)   of a description of property ordinarily intended for private use, occupation or consumption; and

(b)   intended by the person suffering the loss or damage mainly for his own private use, occupation or consumption.

(4)   No damages shall be awarded to any person by virtue of this Part in respect of any loss of or damage to any property if the amount which would fall to be so awarded to that person, apart from this subsection and any liability for interest, does not exceed £275.

(5)   In determining for the purposes of this Part who has suffered any loss of or damage to property and when any such loss or damage occurred, the loss or damage shall be regarded as having occurred at the earliest time at which a person with an interest in the property had knowledge of the material facts about the loss or damage.

(6)   For the purposes of subsection (5) above the material facts about any loss of or damage to any property are such facts about the loss or damage as would lead a reasonable person with an interest in the property to consider the loss or damage sufficiently serious to justify his instituting proceedings for damages against a defendant who did not dispute liability and was able to satisfy a judgment.

(7)   For the purposes of subsection (5) above a person's knowledge includes knowledge which he might reasonably have been expected to acquire—

(a)   from facts observable or ascertainable by him; or

(b)   from facts ascertainable by him with the help of appropriate expert advice which it is reasonable for him to seek;

but a person shall not be taken by virtue of this subsection to have knowledge of a fact ascertainable by him only with the help of expert advice unless he has failed to take all reasonable steps to obtain (and, where appropriate, to act on) that advice.

(8)   Subsections (5) to (7) above shall not extend to Scotland.

Application of certain enactments etc.
6.—(1)   Any damage for which a person is liable under section 2 above shall be deemed to have been caused—

(a)　for the purposes of the Fatal Accidents Act 1976, by that person's wrongful act, neglect or default;

(b)　for the purposes of section 3 of the Law Reform (Miscellaneous Provisions) (Scotland) Act 1940 (contribution among joint wrongdoers), by that person's wrongful act or negligent act or omission;

(c)　for the purposes of section 1 of the Damages (Scotland) Act 1976 (rights of relatives of a deceased), by that person's act or omission; and

(d)　for the purposes of Part II of the Administration of Justice Act 1982 (damages for personal injuries, etc.—Scotland), by an act or omission giving rise to liability in that person to pay damages.

(2)　Where—

(a)　a person's death is caused wholly or partly by a defect in a product, or a person dies after suffering damage which has been so caused;

(b)　a request such as mentioned in paragraph (a) of subsection (3) of section 2 above is made to a supplier of the product by that person's personal representatives or, in the case of a person whose death is caused wholly or partly by the defect, by any dependant or relative of that person; and

(c)　the conditions specified in paragraphs (b) and (c) of that subsection are satisfied in relation to that request,

this Part shall have effect for the purposes of the Law Reform (Miscellaneous Provisions) Act 1934, the Fatal Accidents Act 1976 and the Damages (Scotland) Act 1976 as if liability of the supplier to that person under that subsection did not depend on that person having requested the supplier to identify certain persons or on the said conditions having been satisfied in relation to a request made by that person.

(3)　Section 1 of the Congenital Disabilities (Civil Liability) Act 1976 shall have effect for the purposes of this Part as if—

(a)　a person were answerable to a child in respect of an occurrence caused wholly or partly by a defect in a product if he is or has been liable under section 2 above in respect of any effect of the occurrence on a parent of the child, or would be so liable if the occurrence caused a parent of the child to suffer damage;

(b)　the provisions of this Part relating to liability under section 2 above applied in relation to liability by virtue of paragraph (a) above under the said section 1; and

(c)　subsection (6) of the said section 1 (exclusion of liability) were omitted.

(4)　Where any damage is caused partly by a defect in a product and partly by the fault of the person suffering the damage, the Law Reform (Contributory Negligence) Act 1945 and section 5 of the Fatal Accidents Act 1976 (contributory negligence) shall have effect as if the defect were the fault of every person liable by virtue of this Part for the damage caused by the defect.

(5)　In subsection (4) above 'fault' has the same meaning as in the said Act of 1945.

(6)　Schedule 1 to this Act shall have effect for the purpose of amending the Limitation Act 1980 and the Prescription and Limitation (Scotland) Act 1973 in their application in relation to the bringing of actions by virtue of this Part.

(7)　It is hereby declared that liability by virtue of this Part is to be treated as liability in tort for the purposes of any enactment conferring jurisdiction on any court with respect to any matter.

(8)　Nothing in this Part shall prejudice the operation of section 12 of the Nuclear

Installations Act 1965 (rights to compensation for certain breaches of duties confined to rights under that Act).

Prohibition on exclusions from liability

7. The liability of a person by virtue of this Part to a person who has suffered damage caused wholly or partly by a defect in a product, or to a dependant or relative of such a person, shall not be limited or excluded by any contract term, by any notice or by any other provision.

Power to modify Part I

8.—(1) Her Majesty may by Order in Council make such modifications of this Part and of any other enactment (including an enactment contained in the following Parts of this Act, or in an Act passed after this Act) as appear to Her Majesty in Council to be necessary or expedient in consequence of any modification of the product liability Directive which is made at any time after the passing of this Act.

(2) An Order in Council under subsection (1) above shall not be submitted to Her Majesty in Council unless a draft of the Order has been laid before, and approved by a resolution of, each House of Parliament.

Application of Part I to Crown

9.—(1) Subject to subsection (2) below, this Part shall bind the Crown.

(2) The Crown shall not, as regards the Crown's liability by virtue of this Part, be bound by this Part further than the Crown is made liable in tort or in reparation under the Crown Proceedings Act 1947, as that Act has effect from time to time.

Part II   Consumer Safety

The general safety requirement

10.—(1) A person shall be guilty of an offence if he—

    (a) supplies any consumer goods which fail to comply with the general safety requirement;

    (b) offers or agrees to supply any such goods; or

    (c) exposes or possesses any such goods for supply.

(2) For the purposes of this section consumer goods fail to comply with the general safety requirement if they are not reasonably safe having regard to all the circumstances, including—

    (a) the manner in which, and purposes for which, the goods are being or would be marketed, the get-up of the goods, the use of any mark in relation to the goods and any instructions or warnings which are given or would be given with respect to the keeping, use or consumption of the goods;

    (b) any standards of safety published by any person either for goods of a description which applies to the goods in question or for matters relating to goods of that description; and

    (c) the existence of any means by which it would have been reasonable (taking into account the cost, likelihood and extent of any improvement) for the goods to have been made safer.

(3)   For the purposes of this section consumer goods shall not be regarded as failing to comply with the general safety requirement in respect of—

(a)   anything which is shown to be attributable to compliance with any requirement imposed by or under any enactment or with any Community obligation;

(b)   any failure to do more in relation to any matter than is required by—

(i)   any safety regulations imposing requirements with respect to that matter;

(ii)   any standards of safety approved for the purposes of this subsection by or under any such regulations and imposing requirements with respect to that matter;

(iii)   any provision of any enactment or subordinate legislation imposing such requirements with respect to that matter as are designated for the purposes of this subsection by any such regulations.

(4)   In any proceedings against any person for an offence under this section in respect of any goods it shall be a defence for that person to show—

(a)   that he reasonably believed that the goods would not be used or consumed in the United Kingdom; or

(b)   that the following conditions are satisfied, that is to say—

(i)   that he supplied the goods, offered or agreed to supply them or, as the case may be, exposed or possessed them for supply in the course of carrying on a retail business; and

(ii)   that, at the time he supplied the goods or offered or agreed to supply them or exposed or possessed them for supply, he neither knew nor had reasonable grounds for believing that the goods failed to comply with the general safety requirement; or

(c)   that the terms on which he supplied the goods or agreed or offered to supply them or, in the case of goods which he exposed or possessed for supply, the terms on which he intended to supply them—

(i)   indicated that the goods were not supplied or to be supplied as new goods; and

(ii)   provided for, or contemplated, the acquisition of an interest in the goods by the persons supplied or to be supplied.

(5)   For the purposes of subsection (4)(b) above goods are supplied in the course of carrying on a retail business if—

(a)   whether or not they are themselves acquired for a person's private use or consumption, they are supplied in the course of carrying on a business of making a supply of consumer goods available to persons who generally acquire them for private use or consumption; and

(b)   the descriptions of goods the supply of which is made available in the course of that business do not, to a significant extent, include manufactured or imported goods which have not previously been supplied in the United Kingdom.

(6)   A person guilty of an offence under this section shall be liable on summary conviction to imprisonment for a term not exceeding six months or to a fine not exceeding level 5 on the standard scale or to both.

(7)   In this section 'consumer goods' means any goods which are ordinarily intended for private use or consumption, not being—

    (a)   growing crops or things comprised in land by virtue of being attached to it;

    (b)   water, food, feeding stuff or fertiliser;

    (c)   gas which is, is to be or has been supplied by a person authorised to supply it by or under section 6, 7 or 8 of the Gas Act 1986 (authorisation of supply of gas through pipes);

    (d)   aircraft (other than hang-gliders) or motor vehicles;

    (e)   controlled drugs or licensed medicinal products;

    (f)   tobacco.

Safety regulations

11.—(1) The Secretary of State may by regulations under this section ('safety regulations') make such provision as he considers appropriate for the purposes of section 10(3) above and for the purpose of securing—

    (a)   that goods to which this section applies are safe;

    (b)   that goods to which this section applies which are unsafe, or would be unsafe in the hands of persons of a particular description, are not made available to persons generally or, as the case may be, to persons of that description; and

    (c)   that appropriate information is, and inappropriate information is not, provided in relation to goods to which this section applies.

(2) Without prejudice to the generality of subsection (1) above, safety regulations may contain provision—

    (a)   with respect to the composition or contents, design, construction, finish or packing of goods to which this section applies, with respect to standards for such goods and with respect to other matters relating to such goods;

    (b)   with respect to the giving, refusal, alteration or cancellation of approvals of such goods, of descriptions of such goods or of standards for such goods;

    (c)   with respect to the conditions that may be attached to any approval given under the regulations;

    (d)   for requiring such fees as may be determined by or under the regulations to be paid on the giving or alteration of any approval under the regulations and on the making of an application for such an approval or alteration;

    (e)   with respect to appeals against refusals, alterations and cancellations of approvals given under the regulations and against the conditions contained in such approvals;

    (f)   for requiring goods to which this section applies to be approved under the regulations or to conform to the requirements of the regulations or to descriptions or standards specified in or approved by or under the regulations;

    (g)   with respect to the testing or inspection of goods to which this section applies (including provision for determining the standards to be applied in carrying out any test or inspection);

    (h)   with respect to the ways of dealing with goods of which some or all do not satisfy a test required by or under the regulations or a standard connected with a procedure so required;

    (i)   for requiring a mark, warning or instruction or any other information relating to goods to be put on or to accompany the goods or to be used or provided in some other manner in relation to the goods, and for securing that inappropriate information is not given in relation to goods either by means of misleading marks or otherwise;

(j) for prohibiting persons from supplying, or from offering to supply, agreeing to supply, exposing for supply or possessing for supply, goods to which this section applies and component parts and raw materials for such goods;

(k) for requiring information to be given to any such person as may be determined by or under the regulations for the purpose of enabling that person to exercise any function conferred on him by the regulations.

(3) Without prejudice as aforesaid, safety regulations may contain provision—

(a) for requiring persons on whom functions are conferred by or under section 27 below to have regard, in exercising their functions so far as relating to any provision of safety regulations, to matters specified in a direction issued by the Secretary of State with respect to that provision;

(b) for securing that a person shall not be guilty of an offence under section 12 below unless it is shown that the goods in question do not conform to a particular standard;

(c) for securing that proceedings for such an offence are not brought in England and Wales except by or with the consent of the Secretary of State or the Director of Public Prosecutions;

(d) for securing that proceedings for such an offence are not brought in Northern Ireland except by or with the consent of the Secretary of State or the Director of Public Prosecutions for Northern Ireland;

(e) for enabling a magistrates' court in England and Wales or Northern Ireland to try an information or, in Northern Ireland, a complaint in respect of such an offence if the information was laid or the complaint made within 12 months from the time when the offence was committed;

(f) for enabling summary proceedings for such an offence to be brought in Scotland at any time within 12 months from the time when the offence was committed; and

(g) for determining the persons by whom, and the manner in which, anything required to be done by or under the regulations is to be done.

(4) Safety regulations shall not provide for any contravention of the regulations to be an offence.

(5) Where the Secretary of State proposes to make safety regulations it shall be his duty before he makes them—

(a) to consult such organisations as appear to him to be representative of interests substantially affected by the proposal;

(b) to consult such other persons as he considers appropriate; and

(c) in the case of proposed regulations relating to goods suitable for use at work, to consult the Health and Safety Commission in relation to the application of the proposed regulations to Great Britain;

but the preceding provisions of this subsection shall not apply in the case of regulations which provide for the regulations to cease to have effect at the end of a period of not more than 12 months beginning with the day on which they come into force and which contain a statement that it appears to the Secretary of State that the need to protect the public requires that the regulations should be made without delay.

(6) The power to make safety regulations shall be exercisable by statutory instrument subject to annulment in pursuance of a resolution of either House of Parliament and shall include power—

(a)   to make different provision for different cases; and

(b)   to make such supplemental, consequential and transitional provision as the Secretary of State considers appropriate.

(7)   This section applies to any goods other than—

(a)   growing crops and things comprised in land by virtue of being attached to it;

(b)   water, food, feeding stuff and fertiliser;

(c)   gas which is, is to be or has been supplied by a person authorised to supply it by or under section 6, 7 or 8 of the Gas Act 1986 (authorisation of supply of gas through pipes);

(d)   controlled drugs and licensed medicinal products.

Offences against the safety regulations

12.—(1)   Where safety regulations prohibit a person from supplying or offering or agreeing to supply any goods or from exposing or possessing any goods for supply, that person shall be guilty of an offence if he contravenes the prohibition.

(2)   Where safety regulations require a person who makes or processes any goods in the course of carrying on a business—

(a)   to carry out a particular test or use a particular procedure in connection with the making or processing of the goods with a view to ascertaining whether the goods satisfy any requirements of such regulations; or

(b)   to deal or not to deal in a particular way with a quantity of the goods of which the whole or part does not satisfy such a test or does not satisfy standards connected with such a procedure,

that person shall be guilty of an offence if he does not comply with the requirement.

(3)   If a person contravenes a provision of safety regulations which prohibits or requires the provision, by means of a mark or otherwise, of information of a particular kind in relation to goods, he shall be guilty of an offence.

(4)   Where safety regulations require any person to give information to another for the purpose of enabling that other to exercise any function, that person shall be guilty of an offence if—

(a)   he fails without reasonable cause to comply with the requirement; or

(b)   in giving the information which is required of him—

(i)   he makes any statement which he knows is false in a material particular; or

(ii)   he recklessly makes any statement which is false in a material particular.

(5)   A person guilty of an offence under this section shall be liable on summary conviction to imprisonment for a term not exceeding six months or to a fine not exceeding level 5 on the standard scale or to both.

Prohibition notices and notices to warn

13.—(1)   The Secretary of State may—

    (a)   serve on any person a notice ('a prohibition notice') prohibiting that person, except with the consent of the Secretary of State, from supplying, or from offering to supply, agreeing to supply, exposing for supply or possessing for supply, any relevant goods which the Secretary of State considers are unsafe and which are described in the notice;

    (b)   serve on any person a notice ('a notice to warn') requiring that person at his own expense to publish, in a form and manner and on occasions specified in the notice, a warning about any relevant goods which the Secretary of State considers are unsafe, which that person supplies or has supplied and which are described in the notice.

(2)   Schedule 2 to this Act shall have effect with respect to prohibition notices and notices to warn; and the Secretary of State may by regulations make provision specifying the manner in which information is to be given to any person under that Schedule.

(3)   A consent given by the Secretary of State for the purposes of a prohibition notice may impose such conditions on the doing of anything for which the consent is required as the Secretary of State considers appropriate.

(4)   A person who contravenes a prohibition notice or a notice to warn shall be guilty of an offence and liable on summary conviction to imprisonment for a term not exceeding six months or to a fine not exceeding level 5 on the standard scale or to both.

(5)   The power to make regulations under subsection (2) above shall be exercisable by statutory instrument subject to annulment in pursuance of a resolution of either House of Parliament and shall include power—

    (a)   to make different provision for different cases; and

    (b)   to make such supplemental, consequential and transitional provision as the Secretary of State considers appropriate.

(6)   In this section 'relevant goods' means—

    (a)   in relation to a prohibition notice, any goods to which section 11 above applies; and

    (b)   in relation to a notice to warn, any goods to which that section applies or any growing crops or things comprised in land by virtue of being attached to it.

Suspension notices
14.—(1)   Where an enforcement authority has reasonable grounds for suspecting that any safety provision has been contravened in relation to any goods, the authority may serve a notice ('a suspension notice') prohibiting the person on whom it is served, for such period ending not more than six months after the date of the notice as is specified therein, from doing any of the following things without the consent of the authority, that is to say, supplying the goods, offering to supply them, agreeing to supply them or exposing them for supply.

(2)   A suspension notice served by an enforcement authority in respect of any goods shall—

    (a)   describe the goods in a manner sufficient to identify them;

    (b)   set out the grounds on which the authority suspects that a safety provision has been contravened in relation to the goods; and

    (c)   state that, and the manner in which, the person on whom the notice is served may appeal against the notice under section 15 below.

(3)   A suspension notice served by an enforcement authority for the purpose of prohibiting a person for any period from doing the things mentioned in subsection (1) above in relation to any goods may also require that person to keep the authority informed of the whereabouts throughout that period of any of those goods in which he has an interest.

(4)   Where a suspension notice has been served on any person in respect of any goods, no further such notice shall be served on that person in respect of the same goods unless—

(a)   proceedings against that person for an offence in respect of a contravention in relation to the goods of a safety provision (not being an offence under this section); or

(b)   proceedings for the forfeiture of the goods under section 16 or 17 below,

are pending at the end of the period specified in the first-mentioned notice.

(5)   A consent given by an enforcement authority for the purposes of subsection (1) above may impose such conditions on the doing of anything for which the consent is required as the authority considers appropriate.

(6)   Any person who contravenes a suspension notice shall be guilty of an offence and liable on summary conviction to imprisonment for a term not exceeding six months or to a fine not exceeding level 5 on the standard scale or to both.

(7)   Where an enforcement authority serves a suspension notice in respect of any goods, the authority shall be liable to pay compensation to any person having an interest in the goods in respect of any loss or damage caused by reason of the service of the notice if—

(a)   there has been no contravention in relation to the goods of any safety provision; and

(b)   the exercise of the power is not attributable to any neglect or default by that person.

(8)   Any disputed question as to the right to or the amount of any compensation payable under this section shall be determined by arbitration or, in Scotland, by a single arbiter appointed, failing agreement between the parties, by the sheriff.

Appeals against suspension notices

15.—(1)   Any person having an interest in any goods in respect of which a suspension notice is for the time being in force may apply for an order setting aside the notice.

(2)   An application under this section may be made—

(a)   to any magistrates' court in which proceedings have been brought in England and Wales or Northern Ireland—

(i)   for an offence in respect of a contravention in relation to the goods of any safety provision; or

(ii)   for the forfeiture of the goods under section 16 below;

(b)   where no such proceedings have been so brought, by way of complaint to a magistrates' court; or

(c)   in Scotland, by summary application to the sheriff.

(3)   On an application under this section to a magistrates' court in England and

Wales or Northern Ireland the court shall make an order setting aside the suspension notice only if the court is satisfied that there has been no contravention in relation to the goods of any safety provision.

(4) On an application under this section to the sheriff he shall make an order setting aside the suspension notice only if he is satisfied that at the date of making the order—

(a) proceedings for an offence in respect of a contravention in relation to the goods of any safety provision; or

(b) proceedings for the forfeiture of the goods under section 17 below,

have not been brought or, having been brought, have been concluded.

(5) Any person aggrieved by an order made under this section by a magistrates' court in England and Wales or Northern Ireland, or by a decision of such a court not to make such an order, may appeal against that order or decision—

(a) in England and Wales, to the Crown Court;

(b) in Northern Ireland, to the county court;

and an order so made may contain such provision as appears to the court to be appropriate for delaying the coming into force of the order pending the making and determination of any appeal (including any application under section 111 of the Magistrates' Courts Act 1980 or Article 146 of the Magistrates' Courts (Northern Ireland) Order 1981 (statement of case)).

Forfeiture: England and Wales and Northern Ireland

16.—(1) An enforcement authority in England and Wales or Northern Ireland may apply under this section for an order for the forfeiture of any goods on the grounds that there has been a contravention in relation to the goods of a safety provision.

(2) An application under this section may be made—

(a) where proceedings have been brought in a magistrates' court for an offence in respect of a contravention in relation to some or all of the goods of any safety provision, to that court;

(b) where an application with respect to some or all of the goods has been made to a magistrates' court under section 15 above or section 33 below, to that court; and

(c) where no application for the forfeiture of the goods has been made under paragraph (a) or (b) above, by way of complaint to a magistrates' court.

(3) On an application under this section the court shall make an order for the forfeiture of any goods only if it is satisfied that there has been a contravention in relation to the goods of a safety provision.

(4) For the avoidance of doubt it is declared that a court may infer for the purposes of this section that there has been a contravention in relation to any goods of a safety provision if it is satisfied that any such provision has been contravened in relation to goods which are representative of those goods (whether by reason of being of the same design or part of the same consignment or batch or otherwise).

(5). Any person aggrieved by an order made under this section by a magistrates' court, or by a decision of such a court not to make such an order, may appeal against that order or decision—

(a) in England and Wales, to the Crown Court;

(b)   in Northern Ireland, to the county court;

and an order so made may contain such provision as appears to the court to be appropriate for delaying the coming into force of the order pending the making and determination of any appeal (including any application under section 111 of the Magistrates' Courts Act 1980 or Article 146 of the Magistrates' Courts (Northern Ireland) Order 1981 (statement of case)).

(6)   Subject to subsection (7) below, where any goods are forfeited under this section they shall be destroyed in accordance with such directions as the court may give.

(7)   On making an order under this section a magistrates' court may, if it considers it appropriate to do so, direct that the goods to which the order relates shall (instead of being destroyed) be released, to such person as the court may specify, on condition that that person—

(a)   does not supply those goods to any person otherwise than as mentioned in section 46(7)(a) or (b) below; and

(b)   complies with an order to pay costs or expenses (including any order under section 35 below) which has been made against that person in the proceedings for the order for forfeiture.

Forfeiture: Scotland

17.—(1)   In Scotland a sheriff may make an order for forfeiture of any goods in relation to which there has been a contravention of a safety provision—

(a)   on an application by the procurator-fiscal made in the manner specified in section 310 of the Criminal Procedure (Scotland) Act 1975; or

(b)   where a person is convicted of any offence in respect of any such contravention, in addition to any other penalty which the sheriff may impose.

(2)   The procurator-fiscal making an application under subsection (1)(a) above shall serve on any person appearing to him to be the owner of, or otherwise to have an interest in, the goods to which the application relates a copy of the application, together with a notice giving him the opportunity to appear at the hearing of the application to show cause why the goods should not be forfeited.

(3)   Service under subsection (2) above shall be carried out, and such service may be proved, in the manner specified for citation of an accused in summary proceedings under the Criminal Procedure (Scotland) Act 1975.

(4)   Any person upon whom notice is served under subsection (2) above and any other person claiming to be the owner of, or otherwise to have an interest in, goods to which an application under this section relates shall be entitled to appear at the hearing of the application to show cause why the goods should not be forfeited.

(5)   The sheriff shall not make an order following an application under subsection (1)(a) above—

(a)   if any person on whom notice is served under subsection (2) above does not appear, unless service of the notice on that person is proved; or

(b)   if no notice under subsection (2) above has been served, unless the court is satisfied that in the circumstances it was reasonable not to serve notice on any person.

(6)   The sheriff shall make an order under this section only if he is satisfied that

there has been a contravention in relation to those goods of a safety provision.

(7) For the avoidance of doubt it is declared that the sheriff may infer for the purposes of this section that there has been a contravention in relation to any goods of a safety provision if he is satisfied that any such provision has been contravened in relation to any goods which are representative of those goods (whether by reason of being of the same design or part of the same consignment or batch or otherwise).

(8) Where an order for the forfeiture of any goods is made following an application by the procurator-fiscal under subsection (1)(a) above, any person who appeared, or was entitled to appear, to show cause why goods should not be forfeited may, within 21 days of the making of the order, appeal to the High Court by Bill of Suspension on the ground of an alleged miscarriage of justice; and section 452(4)(a) to (e) of the Criminal Procedure (Scotland) Act 1975 shall apply to an appeal under this subsection as it applies to a stated case under Part II of that Act.

(9) An order following an application under subsection (1)(a) above shall not take effect—

(a) until the end of the period of 21 days beginning with the day after the day on which the order is made; or

(b) if an appeal is made under subsection (8) above within that period, until the appeal is determined or abandoned.

(10) An order under subsection (1)(b) above shall not take effect—

(a) until the end of the period within which an appeal against the order could be brought under the Criminal Procedure (Scotland) Act 1975; or

(b) if an appeal is made within that period, until the appeal is determined or abandoned.

(11) Subject to subsection (12) below, goods forfeited under this section shall be destroyed in accordance with such directions as the sheriff may give.

(12) If he thinks fit, the sheriff may direct that the goods be released, to such person as he may specify, on condition that that person does not supply those goods to any other person otherwise than as mentioned in section 46(7)(a) or (b) below.

Power to obtain information
18.—(1) If the Secretary of State considers that, for the purpose of deciding whether—

(a) to make, vary or revoke any safety regulations; or
(b) to serve, vary or revoke a prohibition notice; or
(c) to serve or revoke a notice to warn,

he requires information which another person is likely to be able to furnish, the Secretary of State may serve on the other person a notice under this section.

(2) A notice served on any person under this section may require that person—

(a) to furnish to the Secretary of State, within a period specified in the notice, such information as is so specified;

(b) to produce such records as are specified in the notice at a time and place so specified and to permit a person appointed by the Secretary of State for the purpose to take copies of the records at that time and place.

(3)   A person shall be guilty of an offence if he—

(a)   fails, without reasonable cause, to comply with a notice served on him under this section; or

(b)   in purporting to comply with a requirement which by virtue of paragraph (a) of subsection (2) above is contained in such a notice—

(i)   furnishes information which he knows is false in a material particular; or

(ii)   recklessly furnishes information which is false in a material particular.

(4)   A person guilty of an offence under subsection (3) above shall—

(a)   in the case of an offence under paragraph (a) of that subsection, be liable on summary conviction to a fine not exceeding level 5 on the standard scale; and

(b)   in the case of an offence under paragraph (b) of that subsection be liable—

(i)   on conviction on indictment, to a fine;

(ii)   on summary conviction, to a fine not exceeding the statutory maximum.

Interpretation of Part II
19.—(1)   In this Part—

'controlled drug' means a controlled drug within the meaning of the Misuse of Drugs Act 1971;

'feeding stuff' and 'fertiliser' have the same meanings as in Part IV of the Agriculture Act 1970;

'food' does not include anything containing tobacco but, subject to that, has the same meaning as in the Food Act 1984 or, in relation to Northern Ireland, the same meaning as in the Food and Drugs Act (Northern Ireland) 1958;

'licensed medicinal product' means—

(a)   any medicinal product within the meaning of the Medicines Act 1968 in respect of which a product licence within the meaning of that Act is for the time being in force; or

(b)   any other article or substance in respect of which any such licence is for the time being in force in pursuance of an order under section 104 or 105 of that Act (application of Act to other articles and substances);

'safe', in relation to any goods, means such that there is no risk, or no risk apart from one reduced to a minimum, that any of the following will (whether immediately or after a definite or indefinite period) cause the death of, or any personal injury to, any person whatsoever, that is to say—

(a)   the goods;

(b)   the keeping, use or consumption of the goods;

(c)   the assembly of any of the goods which are, or are to be, supplied unassembled;

(d)   any emission or leakage from the goods or, as a result of the keeping, use or consumption of the goods, from anything else; or

(e)   reliance on the accuracy of any measurement, calculation or other reading made by or by means of the goods,

and 'safer' and 'unsafe' shall be construed accordingly;

'tobacco' includes any tobacco product within the meaning of the Tobacco Products Duty Act 1979 and any article or substance containing tobacco and intended for oral or nasal use.

(2)   In the definition of 'safe' in subsection (1) above, references to the keeping, use or consumption of any goods are references to—

(a)   the keeping, use or consumption of the goods by the persons by whom, and in all or any of the ways or circumstances in which they might reasonably be expected to be kept, used or consumed; and

(b)   the keeping, use or consumption of the goods either alone or in conjunction with other goods in conjunction with which they might reasonably be expected to be kept, used or consumed.

Part III   Misleading Price Indications

Offence of giving misleading indication

20.—(1)   Subject to the following provisions of this Part, a person shall be guilty of an offence if, in the course of any business of his, he gives (by any means whatever) to any consumers an indication which is misleading as to the price at which any goods, services, accommodation or facilities are available (whether generally or from particular persons).

(2)   Subject as aforesaid, a person shall be guilty of an offence if—

(a)   in the course of any business of his, he has given an indication to any consumers which, after it was given, has become misleading as mentioned in subsection (1) above; and

(b)   some or all of those consumers might reasonably be expected to rely on the indication at a time after it has become misleading; and

(c)   he fails to take all such steps as are reasonable to prevent those consumers from relying on the indication.

(3)   For the purposes of this section it shall be immaterial—

(a)   whether the person who gives or gave the indication is or was acting on his own behalf or on behalf of another;

(b)   whether or not that person is the person, or included among the persons, from whom the goods, services, accommodation or facilities are available; and

(c)   whether the indication is or has become misleading in relation to all the consumers to whom it is or was given or only in relation to some of them.

(4)   A person guilty of an offence under subsection (1) or (2) above shall be liable—

(a)   on conviction on indictment, to a fine;

(b)   on summary conviction, to a fine not exceeding the statutory maximum.

(5)   No prosecution for an offence under subsection (1) or (2) above shall be brought after whichever is the earlier of the following, that is to say—

(a)   the end of the period of three years beginning with the day on which the offence was committed; and

(b)   the end of the period of one year beginning with the day on which the person bringing the prosecution discovered that the offence had been committed.

(6)   In this Part—

'consumer'—

(a)   in relation to any goods, means any person who might wish to be supplied with the goods for his own private use or consumption;

(b)   in relation to any services or facilities, means any person who might wish to be provided with the services or facilities otherwise than for the purposes of any business of his; and

(c)   in relation to any accommodation, means any person who might wish to occupy the accommodation otherwise than for the purposes of any business of his;

'price', in relation to any goods, services, accommodation or facilities, means—

(a)   the aggregate of the sums required to be paid by a consumer for or otherwise in respect of the supply of the goods or the provision of the services, accommodation or facilities; or

(b)   except in section 21 below, any method which will be or has been applied for the purpose of determining that aggregate.

Meaning of 'misleading'

21.—(1)   For the purposes of section 20 above an indication given to any consumers is misleading as to a price if what is conveyed by the indication, or what those consumers might reasonably be expected to infer from the indication or any omission from it, includes any of the following, that is to say—

(a)   that the price is less than in fact it is;

(b)   that the applicability of the price does not depend on facts or circumstances on which its applicability does in fact depend;

(c)   that the price covers matters in respect of which an additional charge is in fact made;

(d)   that a person who in fact has no such expectation—

(i)   expects the price to be increased or reduced (whether or not at a particular time or by a particular amount); or

(ii)   expects the price, or the price as increased or reduced, to be maintained (whether or not for a particular period); or

(e)   that the facts or circumstances by reference to which the consumers might reasonably be expected to judge the validity of any relevant comparison made or implied by the indication are not what in fact they are.

(2)   For the purposes of section 20 above, an indication given to any consumers is misleading as to a method of determining a price if what is conveyed by the indication, or what those consumers might reasonably be expected to infer from the indication or any omission from it, includes any of the following, that is to say—

(a)   that the method is not what in fact it is;

(b)   that the applicability of the method does not depend on facts or circumstances on which its applicability does in fact depend;

(c)   that the method takes into account matters in respect of which an additional charge will in fact be made;

(d)   that a person who in fact has no such expectation—

(i)   expects the method to be altered (whether or not at a particular time or in a particular respect); or

(ii)   expects the method, or that method as altered, to remain unaltered (whether or not for a particular period); or

(e)   that the facts or circumstances by reference to which the consumers might reasonably be expected to judge the validity of any relevant comparison made or implied by the indication are not what in fact they are.

(3)   For the purposes of subsections (1)(e) and (2)(e) above a comparison is a relevant comparison in relation to a price or method of determining a price if it is made between that price or that method, or any price which has been or may be determined by that method, and—

(a)   any price or value which is stated or implied to be, to have been or to be likely to be attributed or attributable to the goods, services, accommodation or facilities in question or to any other goods, services, accommodation or facilities; or

(b)   any method, or other method, which is stated or implied to be, to have been or to be likely to be applied or applicable for the determination of the price or value of the goods, services, accommodation or facilities in question or of the price or value of any other goods, services, accommodation or facilities.

Application to provision of services and facilities
22.—(1)   Subject to the following provisions of this section, references in this Part to services or facilities are references to any services or facilities whatever including, in particular—

(a)   the provision of credit or of banking or insurance services and the provision of facilities incidental to the provision of such services;

(b)   the purchase or sale of foreign currency;

(c)   the supply of electricity;

(d)   the provision of a place, other than on a highway, for the parking of a motor vehicle;

(e)   the making of arrangements for a person to put or keep a caravan on any land other than arrangements by virtue of which that person may occupy the caravan as his only or main residence.

(2)   References in this Part to services shall not include references to services provided to an employer under a contract of employment.

(3)   References in this Part to services or facilities shall not include references to services or facilities which are provided by an authorised person or appointed representative in the course of the carrying on of an investment business.

(4)   In relation to a service consisting in the purchase or sale of foreign currency, references in this Part to the method by which the price of the service is determined shall include references to the rate of exchange.

(5)   In this section—

'appointed representative', 'authorised person' and 'investment business' have the same meanings as in the Financial Services Act 1986;

'caravan' has the same meaning as in the Caravan Sites and Control of Development Act 1960;

'contract of employment' and 'employer' have the same meanings as in the Employment Protection (Consolidation) Act 1978;

'credit' has the same meaning as in the Consumer Credit Act 1974.

Application to provision of accommodation etc.

23.—(1)   Subject to subsection (2) below, references in this Part to accomodation or facilities being available shall not include references to accommodation or facilities being available to be provided by means of the creation or disposal of an interest in land except where—

(a)   the person who is to create or dispose of the interest will do so in the course of any business of his; and

(b)   the interest to be created or disposed of is a relevant interest in a new dwelling and is to be created or disposed of for the purpose of enabling that dwelling to be occupied as a residence, or one of the residences, of the person acquiring the interest.

(2)   Subsection (1) above shall not prevent the application of any provision of this Part in relation to—

(a)   the supply of any goods as part of the same transaction as any creation or disposal of an interest in land; or

(b)   the provisions of any services or facilities for the purposes of, or in connection with, any transaction for the creation or disposal of such an interest.

(3)   In this section—

'new dwelling' means any building or part of a building in Great Britain which—

(a)   has been constructed or adapted to be occupied as a residence; and

(b)   has not previously been so occupied or has been so occupied only with other premises or as more than one residence,

and includes any yard, garden, outhouses or appurtenances which belong to that building or part or are to be enjoyed with it;

'relevant interest'—

(a)   in relation to a new dwelling in England and Wales, means the freehold estate in the dwelling or a leasehold interest in the dwelling for a term of years absolute of more than 21 years, not being a term of which 21 years or less remains unexpired;

(b)   in relation to a new dwelling in Scotland, means the *dominium utile* of the land comprising the dwelling, or a leasehold interest in the dwelling where 21 years or more remains unexpired.

Defences

24.—(1)   In any proceedings against a person for an offence under subsection (1) or (2) of section 20 above in respect of any indication it shall be a defence for that person to show that his acts or omissions were authorised for the purposes of this subsection by regulations made under section 26 below.

(2)　In proceedings against a person for an offence under subsection (1) or (2) of section 20 above in respect of an indication published in a book, newspaper, magazine, film or radio or television broadcast or in a programme included in a cable programme service, it shall be a defence for that person to show that the indication was not contained in an advertisement.

(3)　In proceedings against a person for an offence under subsection (1) or (2) of section 20 above in respect of an indication published in an advertisement it shall be a defence for that person to show that—

(a)　he is a person who carries on a business of publishing or arranging for the publication of advertisements;

(b)　he received the advertisement for publication in the ordinary course of that business; and

(c)　at the time of publication he did not know and had no grounds for suspecting that the publication would involve the commission of the offence.

(4)　In any proceedings against a person for an offence under subsection (1) of section 20 above in respect of any indication, it shall be a defence for that person to show that—

(a)　the indication did not relate to the availability from him of any goods, services, accommodation or facilities;

(b)　a price had been recommended to every person from whom the goods, services, accommodation or facilities were indicated as being available;

(c)　the indication related to that price and was misleading as to that price only by reason of a failure by any person to follow the recommendation; and

(d)　it was reasonable for the person who gave the indication to assume that the recommendation was for the most part being followed.

(5)　The provisions of this section are without prejudice to the provisions of section 39 below.

(6)　In this section—

'advertisement' includes a catalogue, a circular and a price list;

'cable programme service' has the same meaning as in the Cable and Broadcasting Act 1984.

Code of practice

25.—(1)　The Secretary of State may, after consulting the Director General of Fair Trading and such other persons as the Secretary of State considers it appropriate to consult, by order approve any code of practice issued (whether by the Secretary of State or another person) for the purpose of—

(a)　giving practical guidance with respect to any of the requirements of section 20 above; and

(b)　promoting what appear to the Secretary of State to be desirable practices as to the circumstances and manner in which any person gives an indication as to the price at which any goods, services, accommodation or facilities are available or indicates any other matter in respect of which any such indication may be misleading.

(2)　A contravention of a code of practice approved under this section shall not of itself give rise to any criminal or civil liability, but in any proceedings against any person for an offence under section 20(1) or (2) above—

(a)   any contravention by that person of such a code may be relied on in relation to any matter for the purpose of establishing that that person committed the offence or of negativing any defence; and

(b)   compliance by that person with such a code may be relied on in relation to any matter for the purpose of showing that the commission of the offence by that person has not been established or that that person has a defence.

(3)   Where the Secretary of State approves a code of practice under this section he may, after such consultation as is mentioned in subsection (1) above, at any time by order—

(a)   approve any modification of the code; or

(b)   withdraw his approval;

and references in subsection (2) above to a code of practice approved under this section shall be construed accordingly.

(4)   The power to make an order under this section shall be exercisable by statutory instrument subject to annulment in pursuance of a resolution of either House of Parliament.

Power to make regulations

26.—(1)   The Secretary of State may, after consulting the Director General of Fair Trading and such other persons as the Secretary of State considers it appropriate to consult, by regulations make provision—

(a)   for the purpose of regulating the circumstances and manner in which any person—

(i)   gives any indication as to the price at which any goods, services, accommodation or facilities will be or are available or have been supplied or provided; or

(ii)   indicates any other matter in respect of which any such indication may be misleading;

(b)   for the purpose of facilitating the enforcement of the provisions of section 20 above or of any regulations made under this section.

(2)   The Secretary of State shall not make regulations by virtue of subsection (1)(a) above except in relation to—

(a)   indications given by persons in the course of business; and

(b)   such indications given otherwise than in the course of business as—

(i)   are given by or on behalf of persons by whom accommodation is provided to others by means of leases or licences; and

(ii)   relate to goods, services or facilities supplied or provided to those others in connection with the provision of the accommodation.

(3)   Without prejudice to the generality of subsection (1) above, regulations under this section may—

(a)   prohibit an indication as to a price from referring to such matters as may be prescribed by the regulations;

    (b)   require an indication as to a price or other matter to be accompanied or supplemented by such explanation or such additional information as may be prescribed by the regulations;

    (c)   require information or explanations with respect to a price or other matter to be given to an officer of an enforcement authority and to authorise such an officer to require such information or explanations to be given;

    (d)   require any information or explanation provided for the purposes of any regulations made by virtue of paragraph (b) or (c) above to be accurate;

    (e)   prohibit the inclusion in indications as to a price or other matter of statements that the indications are not to be relied upon;

    (f)   provide that expressions used in any indication as to a price or other matter shall be construed in a particular way for the purposes of this Part;

    (g)   provide that a contravention of any provision of the regulations shall constitute a criminal offence punishable—

        (i)   on conviction on indictment by a fine;

        (ii)   on summary conviction, by a fine not exceeding the statutory maximum;

    (h)   apply any provision of this Act which relates to a criminal offence to an offence created by virtue of paragraph (g) above.

(4)   The power to make regulations under this section shall be exercisable by statutory instrument subject to annulment in pursuance of a resolution of either House of Parliament and shall include power—

    (a)   to make different provision for different cases; and

    (b)   to make such supplemental, consequential and transitional provision as the Secretary of State considers appropriate.

(5)   In this section 'lease' includes a sublease and an agreement for a lease and a statutory tenancy (within the meaning of the Landlord and Tenant Act 1985 or the Rent (Scotland) Act 1984).

Part IV   Enforcement of Parts II and III

Enforcement

27.—(1)   Subject to the following provisions of this section—

    (a)   it shall be the duty of every weights and measures authority in Great Britain to enforce within their area the safety provisions and the provisions made by or under Part III of this Act; and

    (b)   it shall be the duty of every district council in Northern Ireland to enforce within their area the safety provisions.

(2)   The Secretary of State may by regulations—

    (a)   wholly or partly transfer any duty imposed by subsection (1) above on a weights and measures authority or a district council in Northern Ireland to such other person who has agreed to the transfer as is specified in the regulations;

(b)   relieve such an authority or council of any such duty so far as it is exercisable in relation to such goods as may be described in the regulations.

(3)   The power to make regulations under subsection (2) above shall be exercisable by statutory instrument subject to annulment in pursuance of a resolution of either House of Parliament and shall include power—

(a)   to make different provision for different cases; and

(b)   to make such supplemental, consequential and transitional provision as the Secretary of State considers appropriate.

(4)   Nothing in this section shall authorise any weights and measures authority, or any person on whom functions are conferred by regulations under subsection (2) above, to bring proceedings in Scotland for an offence.

Test purchases

28.—(1)   An enforcement authority shall have power, for the purpose of ascertaining whether any safety provision or any provision made by or under Part III of this Act has been contravened in relation to any goods, services, accommodation or facilities—

(a)   to make, or to authorise an officer of the authority to make, any purchase of any goods; or

(b)   to secure, or to authorise an officer of the authority to secure, the provision of any services, accommodation or facilities.

(2)   Where—

(a)   any goods purchased under this section by or on behalf of an enforcement authority are submitted to a test; and

(b)   the test leads to—

(i)   the bringing of proceedings for an offence in respect of a contravention in relation to the goods of any safety provision or of any provision made by or under Part III of this Act or for the forfeiture of the goods under section 16 or 17 above; or

(ii)   the serving of a suspension notice in respect of any goods; and

(c)   the authority is requested to do so and it is practicable for the authority to comply with the request,

the authority shall allow the person from whom the goods were purchased or any person who is a party to the proceedings or has an interest in any goods to which the notice relates to have the goods tested.

(3)   The Secretary of State may by regulations provide that any test of goods purchased under this section by or on behalf of an enforcement authority shall—

(a)   be carried out at the expense of the authority in a manner and by a person prescribed by or determined under the regulations; or

(b)   be carried out either as mentioned in paragraph (a) above or by the authority in a manner prescribed by the regulations.

(4)   The power to make regulations under subsection (3) above shall be exercisable by statutory instrument subject to annulment in pursuance of a resolution of either House of Parliament and shall include power—

(a)   to make different provision for different cases; and

(b)   to make such supplemental, consequential and transitional provision as the Secretary of State considers appropriate.

(5)   Nothing in this section shall authorise the acquisition by or on behalf of an enforcement authority of any interest in land.

Powers of search etc.
29.—(1)   Subject to the following provisions of this Part, a duly authorised officer of an enforcement authority may at any reasonable hour and on production, if required, of his credentials exercise any of the powers conferred by the following provisions of this section.

(2)   The officer may, for the purpose of ascertaining whether there has been any contravention of any safety provision or of any provision made by or under Part III of this Act, inspect any goods and enter any premises other than premises occupied only as a person's residence.

(3)   The officer may, for the purpose of ascertaining whether there has been any contravention of any safety provision, examine any procedure (including any arrangements for carrying out a test) connected with the production of any goods.

(4)   If the officer has reasonable grounds for suspecting that any goods are manufactured or imported goods which have not been supplied in the United Kingdom since they were manufactured or imported he may—

(a)   for the purpose of ascertaining whether there has been any contravention of any safety provision in relation to the goods, require any person carrying on a business, or employed in connection with a business, to produce any records relating to the business;

(b)   for the purpose of ascertaining (by testing or otherwise) whether there has been any such contravention, seize and detain the goods;

(c)   take copies of, or of any entry in, any records produced by virtue of paragraph (a) above.

(5)   If the officer has reasonable grounds for suspecting that there has been a contravention in relation to any goods of any safety provision or of any provision made by or under Part III of this Act, he may—

(a)   for the purpose of ascertaining whether there has been any such contravention, require any person carrying on a business, or employed in connection with a business, to produce any records relating to the business;

(b)   for the purposeof ascertaining (by testing or otherwise) whether there has been any such contravention, seize and detain the goods;

(c)   take copies of, or of any entry in, any records produced by virtue of paragraph (a) above.

(6)   The officer may seize and detain—

(a)   any goods or records which he has reasonable grounds for believing may be required as evidence in proceedings for an offence in respect of a contravention of any safety provision or of any provision made by or under Part III of this Act;

(b)   any goods which he has reasonable grounds for suspecting may be liable to be forfeited under section 16 or 17 above.

(7) If and to the extent that it is reasonably necessary to do so to prevent a contravention of any safety provision or of any provision made by or under Part III of this Act, the officer may, for the purpose of exercising his power under subsection (4), (5) or (6) above to seize any goods or records—

(a) require any person having authority to do so to open any container or to open any vending machine; and

(b) himself open or break open any such container or machine where a requirement made under paragraph (a) above in relation to the container or machine has not been complied with.

Provisions supplemental to s. 29

30.—(1) An officer seizing any goods or records under section 29 above shall inform the following persons that the goods or records have been so seized, that is to say—

(a) the person from whom they are seized; and

(b) in the case of imported goods seized on any premises under the control of the Commissioners of Customs and Excise, the importer of those goods (within the meaning of the Customs and Excise Management Act 1979).

(2) If a justice of the peace—

(a) is satisfied by any written information on oath that there are reasonable grounds for believing either—

(i) that any goods or records which any officer has power to inspect under section 29 above are on any premises and that their inspection is likely to disclose evidence that there has been a contravention of any safety provision or of any provision made by or under Part III of this Act; or

(ii) that such a contravention has taken place, is taking place or is about to take place on any premises; and

(b) is also satisfied by any such information either—

(i) that admission to the premises has been or is likely to be refused and that notice of intention to apply for a warrant under this subsection has been given to the occupier; or

(ii) that an application for admission, or the giving of such a notice, would defeat the object of the entry or that the premises are unoccupied or that the occupier is temporarily absent and it might defeat the object of the entry to await his return,

the justice may by warrant under his hand, which shall continue in force for a period of one month, authorise any officer of an enforcement authority to enter the premises, if need be by force.

(3) An officer entering any premises by virtue of section 29 above or a warrant under subsection (2) above may take with him such other persons and such equipment as may appear to him necessary.

(4) On leaving any premises which a person is authorised to enter by a warrant under subsection (2) above, that person shall, if the premises are unoccupied or the occupier is temporarily absent, leave the premises as effectively secured against trespassers as he found them.

(5) If any person who is not an officer of an enforcement authority purports to act

as such under section 29 above or this section he shall be guilty of an offence and liable on summary conviction to a fine not exceeding level 5 on the standard scale.

(6)   Where any goods seized by an officer under section 29 above are submitted to a test, the officer shall inform the persons mentioned in subsection (1) above of the result of the test and, if—

(a)   proceedings are brought for an offence in respect of a contravention in relation to the goods of any safety provision or of any provision made by or under Part III of this Act or for the forfeiture of the goods under section 16 or 17 above, or a suspension notice is served in respect of any goods; and

(b)   the officer is requested to do so and it is practicable to comply with the request,

the officer shall allow any person who is a party to the proceedings or, as the case may be, has an interest in the goods to which the notice relates to have the goods tested.

(7)   The Secretary of State may by regulations provide that any test of goods seized under section 29 above by an officer of an enforcement authority shall—

(a)   be carried out at the expense of the authority in a manner and by a person prescribed by or determined under the regulations; or

(b)   be carried out either as mentioned in paragraph (a) above or by the authority in a manner prescribed by the regulations.

(8)   The power to make regulations under subsection (7) above shall be exercisable by statutory instrument subject to annulment in pursuance of a resolution of either House of Parliament and shall include power—

(a)   to make different provision for different cases; and

(b)   to make such supplemental, consequential and transitional provision as the Secretary of State considers appropriate.

(9)   In the application of this section to Scotland, the reference in subsection (2) above to a justice of the peace shall include a reference to a sheriff and the references to written information on oath shall be construed as references to evidence on oath.

(10)   In the application of this section to Northern Ireland, the references in subsection (2) above to any information on oath shall be construed as references to any complaint on oath.

Power of customs officer to detain goods

31.—(1)   A customs officer may, for the purpose of facilitating the exercise by an enforcement authority or officer of such an authority of any functions conferred on the authority or officer by or under Part II of this Act, or by or under this Part in its application for the purposes of the safety provisions, seize any imported goods and detain them for not more than two working days.

(2)   Anything seized and detained under this section shall be dealt with during the period of its detention in such manner as the Commissioners of Customs and Excise may direct.

(3)   In subsection (1) above the reference to two working days is a reference to a period of 48 hours calculated from the time when the goods in question are seized but disregarding so much of any period as falls on a Saturday or Sunday or on Christmas Day, Good Friday or a day which is a bank holiday under the Banking and Financial

Dealings Act 1971 in the Part of the United Kingdom where the goods are seized.

(4)   In this section and section 32 below 'customs officer' means any officer within the meaning of the Customs and Excise Management Act 1979.

Obstruction of authorised officer
32.—(1)   Any person who—

   (a)   intentionally obstructs any officer of an enforcement authority who is acting in pursuance of any provision of this Part or any customs officer who is so acting; or

   (b)   intentionally fails to comply with any requirement made of him by any officer of an enforcement authority under any provision of this Part; or

   (c)   without reasonable cause fails to give any officer of an enforcement authority who is so acting any other assistance or information which the officer may reasonably require of him for the purposes of the exercise of the officer's functions under any provision of this Part,

shall be guilty of an offence and liable on summary conviction to a fine not exceeding level 5 on the standard scale.

(2)   A person shall be guilty of an offence if, in giving any information which is required of him by virtue of subsection (1)(c) above—

   (a)   he makes any statement which he knows is false in a material particular; or
   (b)   he recklessly makes a statement which is false in a material particular.

(3)   A person guilty of an offence under subsection (2) above shall be liable—

   (a)   on conviction on indictment, to a fine;
   (b)   on summary conviction, to a fine not exceeding the statutory maximum.

Appeals against detention of goods
33.—(1)   Any person having an interest in any goods which are for the time being detained under any provision of this Part by an enforcement authority or by an officer of such an authority may apply for an order requiring the goods to be released to him or to another person.

(2)   An application under this section may be made—

   (a)   to any magistrates' court in which proceedings have been brought in England and Wales or Northern Ireland—

      (i)   for an offence in respect of a contravention in relation to the goods of any safety provision or of any provision made by or under Part III of this Act; or
      (ii)   for the forfeiture of the goods under section 16 above;

   (b)   where no such proceedings have been so brought, by way of complaint to a magistrates' court; or

   (c)   in Scotland, by summary application to the sheriff.

(3)   On application under this section to a magistrates' court or to the sheriff, an order requiring goods to be released shall be made only if the court or sheriff is satisfied—

   (a)   that proceedings—

(i)   for an offence in respect of a contravention in relation to the goods of any safety provision or of any provision made by or under Part III of this Act; or

(ii)   for the forfeiture of the goods under section 16 or 17 above,

have not been brought or, having been brought, have been concluded without the goods being forfeited; and

(b)   where no such proceedings have been brought, that more than six months have elapsed since the goods were seized.

(4)   Any person aggrieved by an order made under this section by a magistrates' court in England and Wales or Northern Ireland, or by a decision of such a court not to make such an order, may appeal against that order or decision—

(a)   in England and Wales, to the Crown Court;

(b)   in Northern Ireland, to the county court;

and an order so made may contain such provision as appears to the court to be appropriate for delaying the coming into force of the order pending the making and determination of any appeal (including any application under section 111 of the Magistrates' Courts Act 1980 or Article 146 of the Magistrates' Courts (Northern Ireland) Order 1981 (statement of case)).

Compensation for seizure and detention

34.—(1)   Where an officer of an enforcement authority exercises any power under section 29 above to seize and detain goods, the enforcement authority shall be liable to pay compensation to any person having an interest in the goods in respect of any loss or damage caused by reason of the exercise of the power if—

(a)   there has been no contravention in relation to the goods of any safety provision or of any provision made by or under Part III of this Act; and

(b)   the exercise of the power is not attributable to any neglect or default by that person.

(2)   Any disputed question as to the right to or the amount of any compensation payable under this section shall be determined by arbitration or, in Scotland, by a single arbiter appointed, failing agreement between the parties, by the sheriff.

Recovery of expenses of enforcement

35.—(1)   This section shall apply where a court—

(a)   convicts a person of an offence in respect of a contravention in relation to any goods of any safety provision or of any provision made by or under Part III of this Act; or

(b)   makes an order under section 16 or 17 above for the forfeiture of any goods.

(2)   The court may (in addition to any other order it may make as to costs or expenses) order the person convicted or, as the case may be, any person having an interest in the goods to reimburse an enforcement authority for any expenditure which has been or may be incurred by that authority—

(a)   in connection with any seizure or detention of the goods by or on behalf of the authority; or

(b)   in connection with any compliance by the authority with directions given by the court for the purposes of any order for the forfeiture of the goods.

Part V   Miscellaneous and Supplemental

Amendments of Part I of the Health and Safety at Work etc. Act 1974

36.   Part I of the Health and Safety at Work etc. Act 1974 (which includes provision with respect to the safety of certain articles and substances) shall have effect with the amendments specified in Schedule 3 to this Act; and, accordingly, the general purposes of that Part of that Act shall include the purpose of protecting persons from the risks protection from which would not be afforded by virtue of that Part but for those amendments.

Power of Commissioners of Customs and Excise to disclose information

37.—(1)   If they think it appropriate to do so for the purpose of facilitating the exercise by any person to whom subsection (2) below applies of any functions conferred on that person by or under Part II of this Act, or by or under Part IV of this Act in its application for the purposes of the safety provisions, the Commissioners of Customs and Excise may authorise the disclosure to that person of any information obtained for the purposes of the exercise by the Commissioners of their functions in relation to imported goods.

(2)   This subsection applies to an enforcement authority and to any officer of an enforcement authority.

(3)   A disclosure of information made to any person under subsection (1) above shall be made in such manner as may be directed by the Commissioners of Customs and Excise and may be made through such persons acting on behalf of that person as may be so directed.

(4)   Information may be disclosed to a person under subsection (1) above whether or not the disclosure of the information has been requested by or on behalf of that person.

Restrictions on disclosure of information

38.—(1)   Subject to the following provisions of this section, a person shall be guilty of an offence if he discloses any information—

(a)   which was obtained by him in consequence of its being given to any person in compliance with any requirement imposed by safety regulations or regulations under section 26 above;

(b)   which consists in a secret manufacturing process or a trade secret and was obtained by him in consequence of the inclusion of the information—

(i)   in written or oral representations made for the purposes of Part I or II of Schedule 2 to this Act; or

(ii)   in a statement of a witness in connection with any such oral representations;

(c)   which was obtained by him in consequence of the exercise by the Secretary of State of the power conferred by section 18 above;

(d)   which was obtained by him in consequence of the exercise by any person of any power conferred by Part IV of this Act; or

(e)   which was disclosed to or through him under section 37 above.

(2)   Subsection (1) above shall not apply to a disclosure of information if the information is publicised information or the disclosure is made—

(a)   for the purpose of facilitating the exercise of a relevant person's functions under this Act or any enactment or subordinate legislation mentioned in subsection (3) below;

(b)   for the purposes of compliance with a Community obligation; or

(c)   in connection with the investigation of any criminal offence or for the purposes of any civil or criminal proceedings.

(3)   The enactments and subordinate legislation referred to in subsection (2)(a) above are—

(a)   the Trade Descriptions Act 1968;

(b)   Parts II and III and section 125 of the Fair Trading Act 1973;

(c)   the relevant statutory provisions within the meaning of Part I of the Health and Safety at Work etc. Act 1974 or within the meaning of the Health and Safety at Work (Northern Ireland) Order 1978;

(d)   the Consumer Credit Act 1974;

(e)   the Restrictive Trade Practices Act 1976;

(f)   the Resale Prices Act 1976;

(g)   the Estate Agents Act 1979;

(h)   the Competition Act 1980;

(i)   the Telecommunications Act 1984;

(j)   the Airports Act 1986;

(k)   the Gas Act 1986;

(l)   any subordinate legislation made (whether before or after the passing of this Act) for the purpose of securing compliance with the Directive of the Council of the European Communities, dated 10th September 1984 (No. 84/450/EEC) on the approximation of the laws, regulations and administrative provisions of the member States concerning misleading advertising.

(4)   In subsection (2)(a) above the reference to a person's functions shall include a reference to any function of making, amending or revoking any regulations or order.

(5)   A person guilty of an offence under this section shall be liable—

(a)   on summary conviction, to a fine not exceeding the statutory maximum;

(b)   on conviction on indictment, to imprisonment for a term not exceeding two years or to a fine or to both.

(6)   In this section—

'publicised information' means any information which has been disclosed in any civil or criminal proceedings or is or has been required to be contained in a warning published in pursuance of a notice to warn; and

'relevant person' means any of the following, that is to say—

(a)   a Minister of the Crown, Government department or Northern Ireland department;

(b)   the Monopolies and Mergers Commission, the Director General of Fair

Trading, the Director General of Telecommunications or the Director General of Gas Supply;

    (c)   the Civil Aviation Authority;

    (d)   any weights and measures authority, any district council in Northern Ireland or any person on whom functions are conferred by regulations under section 27(2) above;

    (e)   any person who is an enforcing authority for the purposes of Part I of the Health and Safety at Work etc. Act 1974 or for the purposes of Part II of the Health and Safety at Work (Northern Ireland) Order 1978.

Defence of due diligence

39.—(1) Subject to the following provisions of this section, in proceedings against any person for an offence to which this section applies it shall be a defence for that person to show that he took all reasonable steps and exercised all due diligence to avoid committing the offence.

    (2) Where in any proceedings against any person for such an offence the defence provided by subsection (1) above involves an allegation that the commission of the offence was due—

    (a)   to the act or default of another; or

    (b)   to reliance on information given by another,

that person shall not, without the leave of the court, be entitled to rely on the defence unless, not less than seven clear days before the hearing of the proceedings, he has served a notice under subsection (3) below on the person bringing the proceedings.

    (3) A notice under this subsection shall give such information identifying or assisting in the identification of the person who committed the act or default or gave the information as is in the possession of the person serving the notice at the time he serves it.

    (4) It is hereby declared that a person shall not be entitled to rely on the defence provided by subsection (1) above by reason of his reliance on information supplied by another, unless he shows that it was reasonable in all the circumstances for him to have relied on the information, having regard in particular—

    (a)   to the steps which he took, and those which might reasonably have been taken, for the purpose of verifying the information; and

    (b)   to whether he had any reason to disbelieve the information.

    (5) This section shall apply to an offence under section 10, 12(1), (2) or (3), 13(4), 14(6) or 20(1) above.

Liability of persons other than principal offender

40.—(1) Where the commission by any person of an offence to which section 39 above applies is due to an act or default committed by some other person in the course of any business of his, the other person shall be guilty of the offence and may be proceeded against and punished by virtue of this subsection whether or not proceedings are taken against the first-mentioned person.

    (2) Where a body corporate is guilty of an offence under this Act (including where it is so guilty by virtue of subsection (1) above) in respect of any act or default which is shown to have been committed with the consent or connivance of, or to be attributable

to any neglect on the part of, any director, manager, secretary or other similar officer of the body corporate or any person who was purporting to act in any such capacity he, as well as the body corporate, shall be guilty of that offence and shall be liable to be proceeded against and punished accordingly.

(3)   Where the affairs of a body corporate are managed by its members, subsection (2) above shall apply in relation to the acts and defaults of a member in connection with his functions of management as if he were a director of the body corporate.

Civil proceedings

41.—(1)   An obligation imposed by safety regulations shall be a duty owed to any person who may be affected by a contravention of the obligation and, subject to any provision to the contrary in the regulations and to the defences and other incidents applying to actions for breach of statutory duty, a contravention of any such obligation shall be actionable accordingly.

(2)   This Act shall not be construed as conferring any other right of action in civil proceedings, apart from the right conferred by virtue of Part I of this Act, in respect of any loss or damage suffered in consequence of a contravention of a safety provision or of a provision made by or under Part III of this Act.

(3)   Subject to any provision to the contrary in the agreement itself, an agreement shall not be void or unenforceable by reason only of a contravention of a safety provision or of a provision made by or under Part III of this Act.

(4)   Liability by virtue of subsection (1) above shall not be limited or excluded by any contract term, by any notice or (subject to the power contained in subsection (1) above to limit or exclude it in safety regulations) by any other provision.

(5)   Nothing in subsection (1) above shall prejudice the operation of section 12 of the Nuclear Installations Act 1965 (rights to compensation for certain breaches of duties confined to rights under that Act).

(6)   In this section 'damage' includes personal injury and death.

Reports etc.

42.—(1)   It shall be the duty of the Secretary of State at least once in every five years to lay before each House of Parliament a report on the exercise during the period to which the report relates of the functions which under Part II of this Act, or under Part IV of this Act in its application for the purposes of the safety provisions, are exercisable by the Secretary of State, weights and measures authorities, district councils in Northern Ireland and persons on whom functions are conferred by regulations made under section 27(2) above.

(2)   The Secretary of State may from time to time prepare and lay before each House of Parliament such other reports on the exercise of those functions as he considers appropriate.

(3)   Every weights and measures authority, every district council in Northern Ireland and every person on whom functions are conferred by regulations under subsection (2) of section 27 above shall, whenever the Secretary of State so directs, make a report to the Secretary of State on the exercise of the functions exercisable by that authority or council under that section or by that person by virtue of any such regulations.

(4)   A report under subsection (3) above shall be in such form and shall contain such particulars as are specified in the direction of the Secretary of State.

(5)   The first report under subsection (1) above shall be laid before each House of Parliament not more than five years after the laying of the last report under section 8(2) of the Consumer Safety Act 1978.

Financial provisions

43.—(1)   There shall be paid out of money provided by Parliament—

(a)   any expenses incurred or compensation payable by a Minister of the Crown or Government department in consequence of any provision of this Act; and

(b)   any increase attributable to this Act in the sums payable out of money so provided under any other Act.

(2)   Any sums received by a Minister of the Crown or Government department by virtue of this Act shall be paid into the Consolidated Fund.

Service of documents etc.

44.—(1)   Any document required or authorised by virtue of this Act to be served on a person may be so served—

(a)   by delivering it to him or by leaving it at his proper address or by sending it by post to him at that address; or

(b)   if the person is a body corporate, by serving it in accordance with paragraph (a) above on the secretary or clerk of that body; or

(c)   if the person is a partnership, by serving it in accordance with that paragraph on a partner or on a person having control or management of the partnership business.

(2)   For the purposes of subsection (1) above, and for the purposes of section 7 of the Interpretation Act 1978 (which relates to the service of documents by post) in its application to that subsection, the proper address of any person on whom a document is to be served by virtue of this Act shall be his last known address except that—

(a)   in the case of service on a body corporate or its secretary or clerk, it shall be the address of the registered or principal office of the body corporate;

(b)   in the case of service on a partnership or a partner or a person having the control or management of a partnership business, it shall be the principal office of the partnership;

and for the purposes of this subsection the principal office of a company registered outside the United Kingdom or of a partnership carrying on business outside the United Kingdom is its principal office within the United Kingdom.

(3)   The Secretary of State may by regulations make provision for the manner in which any information is to be given to any person under any provision of Part IV of this Act.

(4)   Without prejudice to the generality of subsection (3) above regulations made by the Secretary of State may prescribe the person, or manner of determining the person, who is to be treated for the purposes of section 28(2) or 30 above as the person from whom any goods were purchased or seized where the goods were purchased or seized from a vending machine.

(5)   The power to make regulations under subsection (3) or (4) above shall be exercisable by statutory instrument subject to annulment in pursuance of a resolution of either House of Parliament and shall include power—

(a)　to make different provision for different cases; and

(b)　to make such supplemental, consequential and transitional provision as the Secretary of State considers appropriate.

Interpretation

45.—(1)　In this Act, except in so far as the context otherwise requires—

'aircraft' includes gliders, balloons and hovercraft;

'business' includes a trade or profession and the activities of a professional or trade association or of a local authority or other public authority;

'conditional sale agreement', 'credit sale agreement' and 'hire-purchase agreement' have the same meanings as in the Consumer Credit Act 1974 but as if in the definitions in that Act 'goods' had the same meaning as in this Act;

'contravention' includes a failure to comply and cognate expressions shall be construed accordingly;

'enforcement authority' means the Secretary of State, any other Minister of the Crown in charge of a Government department, any such department and any authority, council or other person on whom functions under this Act are conferred by or under section 27 above;

'gas' has the same meaning as in Part I of the Gas Act 1986;

'goods' includes substances, growing crops and things comprised in land by virtue of being attached to it and any ship, aircraft or vehicle;

'information' includes accounts, estimates and returns;

'magistrates' court', in relation to Northern Ireland, means a court of summary jurisdiction;

'mark' and 'trade mark' have the same meanings as in the Trade Marks Act 1938;

'modifications' includes additions, alterations and omissions, and cognate expressions shall be construed accordingly;

'motor vehicle' has the same meaning as in the Road Traffic Act 1972;

'notice' means a notice in writing;

'notice to warn' means a notice under section 13(1)(b) above;

'officer', in relation to an enforcement authority, means a person authorised in writing to assist the authority in carrying out its functions under or for the purposes of the enforcement of any of the safety provisions or of any of the provisions made by or under Part III of this Act;

'personal injury' includes any disease and any other impairment of a person's physical or mental condition;

'premises' includes any place and any ship, aircraft or vehicle;

'prohibition notice' means a notice under section 13(1)(a) above;

'records' includes any books or documents and any records in non-documentary form;

'safety provision' means the general safety requirement in section 10 above or any provision of safety regulations, a prohibition notice or a suspension notice;

'safety regulations' means regulations under section 11 above;

'ship' includes any boat and any other description of vessel used in navigation;

'subordinate legislation' has the same meaning as in the Interpretation Act 1978;

'substance' means any natural or artificial substance, whether in solid, liquid or gaseous form or in the form of a vapour, and includes substances that are comprised in or mixed with other goods;

'supply' and cognate expressions shall be construed in accordance with section 46 below;

'suspension notice' means a notice under section 14 above.

(2)   Except in so far as the context otherwise requires, references in this Act to a contravention of a safety provision shall, in relation to any goods, include references to anything which would constitute such a contravention if the goods were supplied to any person.

(3)   References in this Act to any goods in relation to which any safety provision has been or may have been contravened shall include references to any goods which it is not reasonably practicable to separate from any such goods.

(4)   Section 68(2) of the Trade Marks Act 1938 (construction of references to use of a mark) shall apply for the purposes of this Act as it applies for the purposes of that Act.

(5)   In Scotland, any reference in this Act to things comprised in land by virtue of being attached to it is a reference to movables which have become heritable by accession to heritable property.

Meaning of 'supply'

46.—(1)   Subject to the following provisions of this section, references in this Act to supplying goods shall be construed as references to doing any of the following, whether as principal or agent, that is to say—

(a)   selling, hiring out or lending the goods;

(b)   entering into a hire-purchase agreement to furnish the goods;

(c)   the performance of any contract for work and materials to furnish the goods;

(d)   providing the goods in exchange for any consideration (including trading stamps) other than money;

(e)   providing the goods in or in connection with the performance of any statutory function; or

(f)   giving the goods as a prize or otherwise making a gift of the goods;

and, in relation to gas or water, those references shall be construed as including references to providing the service by which the gas or water is made available for use.

(2)   For the purposes of any reference in this Act to supplying goods, where a person ('the ostensible supplier') supplies goods to another person ('the customer') under a hire-purchase agreement, conditional sale agreement or credit-sale agreement or under an agreement for the hiring of goods (other than a hire-purchase agreement) and the ostensible supplier—

(a)   carries on the business of financing the provision of goods for others by means of such agreements; and

(b)   in the course of that business acquired his interest in the goods supplied to the customer as a means of financing the provision of them for the customer by a further person ('the effective supplier'),

the effective supplier and not the ostensible supplier shall be treated as supplying the goods to the customer.

(3)   Subject to subsection (4) below, the performance of any contract by the erection of any building or structure on any land or by the carrying out of any other building

works shall be treated for the purposes of this Act as a supply of goods in so far as, but only in so far as, it involves the provision of any goods to any person by means of their incorporation into the building, structure or works.

(4)   Except for the purposes of, and in relation to, notices to warn or any provision made by or under Part III of this Act, references in this Act to supplying goods shall not include references to supplying goods comprised in land where the supply is effected by the creation or disposal of an interest in the land.

(5)   Except in Part I of this Act references in this Act to a person's supplying goods shall be confined to references to that person's supplying goods in the course of a business of his, but for the purposes of this subsection it shall be immaterial whether the business is a business of dealing in the goods.

(6)   For the purposes of subsection (5) above goods shall not be treated as supplied in the course of a business if they are supplied, in pursuance of an obligation arising under or in connection with the insurance of the goods, to the person with whom they were insured.

(7)   Except for the purposes of, and in relation to, prohibition notices or suspension notices, references in Parts II to IV of this Act to supplying goods shall not include—

(a)   references to supplying goods where the person supplied carries on a business of buying goods of the same description as those goods and repairing or reconditioning them;

(b)   references to supplying goods by a sale of articles as scrap (that is to say, for the value of materials included in the articles rather than for the value of the articles themselves).

(8)   Where any goods have at any time been supplied by being hired out or lent to any person, neither a continuation or renewal of the hire or loan (whether on the same or different terms) nor any transaction for the transfer after that time of any interest in the goods to the person to whom they were hired or lent shall be treated for the purposes of this Act as a further supply of the goods to that person.

(9)   A ship, aircraft or motor vehicle shall not be treated for the purposes of this Act as supplied to any person by reason only that services consisting in the carriage of goods or passengers in that ship, aircraft or vehicle, or in its use for any other purpose, are provided to that person in pursuance of an agreement relating to the use of the ship, aircraft or vehicle for a particular period or for particular voyages, flights or journeys.

Savings for certain privileges

47.—(1)   Nothing in this Act shall be taken as requiring any person to produce any records if he would be entitled to refuse to produce those records in any proceedings in any court on the grounds that they are the subject of legal professional privilege or, in Scotland, that they contain a confidential communication made by or to an advocate or solicitor in that capacity, or as authorising any person to take possession of any records which are in the possession of a person who would be so entitled.

(2)   Nothing in this Act shall be construed as requiring a person to answer any question or give any information if to do so would incriminate that person or that person's spouse.

Minor and consequential amendments and repeals

48.—(1)   The enactments mentioned in Schedule 4 to this Act shall have effect subject to the amendments specified in that Schedule (being minor amendments and amendments consequential on the provisions of this Act).

(2) The following Acts shall cease to have effect, that is to say—

    (a)   the Trade Descriptions Act 1972; and

    (b)   the Fabrics (Misdescription) Act 1913.

(3) The enactments mentioned in Schedule 5 to this Act are hereby repealed to the extent specified in the third column of that Schedule.

Northern Ireland

49.—(1)   This Act shall extend to Northern Ireland with the exception of—

    (a)   the provisions of Parts I and III;

    (b)   any provision amending or repealing an enactment which does not so extend; and

    (c)   any other provision so far as it has effect for the purposes of, or in relation to, a provision falling within paragraph (a) or (b) above.

(2)   Subject to any Order in Council made by virtue of subsection (1)(a) of section 3 of the Northern Ireland Constitution Act 1973, consumer safety shall not be a transferred matter for the purposes of that Act but shall for the purposes of subsection (2) of that section be treated as specified in Schedule 3 to that Act.

(3)   An Order in Council under paragraph 1(1)(b) of Schedule 1 to the Northern Ireland Act 1974 (exercise of legislative functions for Northern Ireland) which states that it is made only for purposes corresponding to any of the provisions of this Act mentioned in subsection (1)(a) to (c) above—

    (a)   shall not be subject to paragraph 1(4) and (5) of that Schedule (affirmative resolution procedure and procedure in cases of urgency); but

    (b)   shall be subject to annulment in pursuance of a resolution of either House of Parliament.

Short title, commencement and transitional provision

50.—(1)   This Act may be cited as the Consumer Protection Act 1987.

(2)   This Act shall come into force on such day as the Secretary of State may by order made by statutory instrument appoint, and different days may be so appointed for different provisions or for different purposes.

(3)   The Secretary of State shall not make an order under subsection (2) above bringing into force the repeal of the Trade Descriptions Act 1972, a repeal of any provision of that Act or a repeal of that Act or of any provision of it for any purposes, unless a draft of the order has been laid before, and approved by a resolution of, each House of Parliament.

(4)   An order under subsection (2) above bringing a provision into force may contain such transitional provision in connection with the coming into force of that provision as the Secretary of State considers appropriate.

(5)   Without prejudice to the generality of the power conferred by subsection (4) above, the Secretary of State may by order provide for any regulations made under the Consumer Protection Act 1961 or the Consumer Protection Act (Northern Ireland) 1965 to have effect as if made under section 11 above and for any such regulations to have effect with such modifications as he considers appropriate for that purpose.

(6)   The power of the Secretary of State by order to make such provision as is mentioned in subsection (5) above, shall, in so far as it is not exercised by an order under subsection (2) above, be exercisable by statutory instrument subject to annulment in pursuance of a resolution of either House of Parliament.

(7)   Nothing in this Act or in any order under subsection (2) above shall make any person liable by virtue of Part I of this Act for any damage caused wholly or partly by a defect in a product which was supplied to any person by its producer before the coming into force of Part I of this Act.

(8)   Expressions used in subsection (7) above and in Part I of this Act have the same meanings in that subsection as in that Part.

Schedule I   Limitation of Actions under Part I

Part I   England and Wales

1.   After section 11 of the Limitation Act 1980 (actions in respect of personal injuries) there shall be inserted the following section—

Actions in respect of defective products
11A.—(1)   This section shall apply to an action for damages by virtue of any provision of Part I of the Consumer Protection Act 1987.

(2)   None of the time-limits given in the preceding provisions of this Act shall apply to an action to which this section applies.

(3)   An action to which this section applies shall not be brought after the expiration of the period of 10 years from the relevant time, within the meaning of section 4 of the said Act of 1987; and this subsection shall operate to extinguish a right of action and shall do so whether or not that right of action had accrued, or time under the following provisions of this Act had begun to run, at the end of the said period of 10 years.

(4)   Subject to subsection (5) below, an action to which this section applies in which the damages claimed by the plaintiff consist of or include damages in respect of personal injuries to the plaintiff or any other person or loss of or damage to any property, shall not be brought after the expiration of the period of three years from whichever is the later of—

(a)   the date on which the cause of action accrued; and

(b)   the date of knowledge of the injured person or, in the case of loss of or damage to property, the date of knowledge of the plaintiff or (if earlier) of any person in whom his cause of action was previously vested.

(5)   If in a case where the damages claimed by the plaintiff consist of or include damages in respect of personal injuries to the plaintiff or any other person the injured person died before the expiration of the period mentioned in subsection (4) above, that subsection shall have effect as respects the cause of action surviving for the benefit of his estate by virtue of section 1 of the Law Reform (Miscellaneous Provisions) Act 1934 as if for the reference to that period there were substituted a reference to the period of three years from whichever is the later of—

(a)   the date of death; and

(b)   the date of the personal representative's knowledge.

(6)   For the purposes of this section "personal representative" includes any person who is or has been a personal representative of the deceased, including an executor who has not proved the will (whether or not he has renounced probate) but not anyone appointed only as a special personal representative in relation to settled land; and regard shall be had to any knowledge acquired by any such person while a personal representative or previously.

(7)   If there is more than one personal representative and their dates of knowledge are different, subsection (5)(b) above shall be read as referring to the earliest of those dates.

(8)   Expressions used in this section or section 14 of this Act and in Part I of the Consumer Protection Act 1987 have the same meanings in this section or that section as in that Part; and section 1(1) of that Act (Part I to be construed as enacted for the purpose of complying with the product liability Directive) shall apply for the purpose of construing this section and the following provisions of this Act so far as they relate to an action by virtue of any provision of that Part as it applies for the purpose of construing that Part.'

2.   In section 12(1) of the said Act of 1980 (actions under the Fatal Accidents Act 1976), after the words 'section 11' there shall be inserted the words 'or 11A'.

3.   In section 14 of the said Act of 1980 (definition of date of knowledge), in subsection (1), at the beginning there shall be inserted the words 'Subject to subsection (1A) below,' and after that subsection there shall be inserted the following subsection—

'(1A)   In section 11A of this Act and in section 12 of this Act so far as that section applies to an action by virtue of section 6(1)(a) of the Consumer Protection Act 1987 (death caused by defective product) references to a person's date of knowledge are references to the date on which he first had knowledge of the following facts—

(a)   such facts about the damage caused by the defect as would lead a reasonable person who had suffered such damage to consider it sufficiently serious to justify his instituting proceedings for damages against a defendant who did not dispute liability and was able to satisfy a judgment; and

(b)   that the damage was wholly or partly attributable to the facts and circumstances alleged to constitute the defect; and

(c)   the identity of the defendant;

but, in determining the date on which a person first had such knowledge there shall be disregarded both the extent (if any) of that person's knowledge on any date of whether particular facts or circumstances would or would not, as a matter of law, constitute a defect and, in a case relating to loss of or damage to property, any knowledge which that person had on a date on which he had no right of action by virtue of Part I of that Act in respect of the loss or damage.'

4.   In section 28 of the said Act of 1980 (extension of limitation period in case of disability), after subsection (6) there shall be inserted the following subsection—

'(7)   If the action is one to which section 11A of this Act applies or one by virtue of section 6(1)(a) of the Consumer Protection Act 1987 (death caused by defective product), subsection (1) above—

(a)   shall not apply to the time-limit prescribed by subsection (3) of the said section 11A or to that time-limit as applied by virtue of section 12(1) of this Act; and

(b)   in relation to any other time-limit prescribed by this Act shall have effect as if for the words "six years" there were substituted the words "three years".'

5.   In section 32 of the said Act of 1980 (postponement of limitation period in case of fraud, concealment or mistake)—

(a)   in subsection (1), for the words 'subsection (3)' there shall be substituted the words 'subsections (3) and (4A)'; and

(b)   after subsection (4) there shall be inserted the following subsection—

'(4A)   Subsection (1) above shall not apply in relation to the time-limit prescribed by section 11A(3) of this Act or in relation to that time-limit as applied by virtue of section 12(1) of this Act.'

6.   In section 33 of the said Act of 1980 (discretionary exclusion of time-limit)—

(a)   in subsection (1), after the words 'section 11' there shall be inserted the words 'or 11A';

(b)   after the said subsection (1) there shall be inserted the following subsection—

'(1A)   The court shall not under this section disapply—

(a)   subsection (3) of section 11A; or

(b)   where the damages claimed by the plaintiff are confined to damages for loss of or damage to any property, any other provision in its application to an action by virtue of Part I of the Consumer Protection Act 1987.';

(c)   in subsections (2) and (4), after the words 'section 11' there shall be inserted the words 'or subsection (4) of section 11A';

(d)   in subsection (3)(b), after the words 'section 11' there shall be inserted the words, 'by section 11A'; and

(e)   in subsection (8), after the words 'section 11' there shall be inserted the words 'or 11A'.

Part II   Scotland

7.   The Prescription and Limitation (Scotland) Act 1973 shall be amended as follows.

8.   In section 7(2), after the words 'not being an obligation' there shall be inserted the words 'to which section 22A of this Act applies or an obligation'.

9.   In Part II, before section 17, there shall be inserted the following section—

'Part II not to extend to product liability
16A.—This Part of this Act does not apply to any action to which section 22B or 22C of this Act applies.'

10.   After section 22, there shall be inserted the following new Part—

'Part IIA   Prescription of Obligations and Limitation of Actions under Part I of
the Consumer Protection Act 1987

Prescription of Obligations

Ten years' prescription of obligations

22A.—(1)   An obligation arising from liability under section 2 of the 1987 Act (to
make reparation for damage caused wholly or partly by a defect in a product) shall
be extinguished if a period of 10 years has expired from the relevant time, unless a
relevant claim was made within that period and has not been finally disposed of,
and no such obligation shall come into existence after the expiration of the said
period.

(2)   If, at the expiration of the period of 10 years mentioned in subsection (1)
above, a relevant claim has been made but has not been finally disposed of, the
obligation to which the claim relates shall be extinguished when the claim is finally
disposed of.

(3)   In this section—

(a)   a decision disposing of the claim has been made against which no
appeal is competent;

(b)   an appeal against such a decision is competent with leave, and the time-
limit for leave has expired and no application has been made or leave has been
refused;

(c)   leave to appeal against such a decision is granted or is not required, and
no appeal is made within the time-limit for appeal; or

(d)   the claim is abandoned.

a claim is finally disposed of when "relevant claim" in relation to an obligation
means a claim made by or on behalf of the creditor for implement or part implement
of the obligation, being a claim made—

(a)   in appropriate proceedings within the meaning of section 4(2) of this
Act; or

(b)   by the presentation of, or the concurring in, a petition for sequestration
or by the submission of a claim under section 22 or 48 of the Bankruptcy (Scotland)
Act 1985; or

(c)   by the presentation of, or the concurring in, a petition for the winding
up of a company or by the submission of a claim in a liquidation in accordance with
the rules made under section 411 of the Insolvency Act 1986;

"relevant time" has the meaning given in section 4(2) of the 1987 Act.

(4)   Where a relevant claim is made in an arbitration, and the nature of the claim
has been stated in a preliminary notice (within the meaning of section 4(4) of this
Act) relating to that arbitration, the date when the notice is served shall be taken for
those purposes to be the date of the making of the claim.

Limitation of actions

Three-year limitation of actions
22B—(1) This section shall apply to an action to enforce an obligation arising from liability under section 2 of the 1987 Act (to make reparation for damage caused wholly or partly by a defect in a product), except where section 22C of this Act applies.

(2) Subject to subsection (4) below, an action to which this section applies shall not be competent unless it is commenced within the period of three years after the earliest date on which the person seeking to bring (or a person who could at an earlier date have brought) the action was aware, or on which, in the opinion of the court, it was reasonably practicable for him in all the circumstances to become aware, of all the facts mentioned in subsection (3) below.

(3) The facts referred to in subsection (2) above are—

(a) that there was a defect in a product;

(b) that the damage was caused or partly caused by the defect;

(c) that the damage was sufficiently serious to justify the pursuer (or other person referred to in subsection (2) above) in bringing an action to which this section applies on the assumption that the defender did not dispute liability and was able to satisfy a decree;

(d) that the defender was a person liable for the damage under the said section 2.

(4) In the computation of the period of three years mentioned in subsection (2) above, there shall be disregarded any period during which the person seeking to bring the action was under legal disability by reason of nonage or unsoundness of mind.

(5) The facts mentioned in subsection (3) above do not include knowledge of whether particular facts and circumstances would or would not, as a matter of law, result in liability for damage under the said section 2.

(6) Where a person would be entitled, but for this section, to bring an action for reparation other than one in which the damages claimed are confined to damages for loss of or damage to property, the court may, if it seems to it equitable to do so, allow him to bring the action notwithstanding this section.

Actions under the 1987 Act where death has resulted from personal injuries
22C.—(1) This section shall apply to an action to enforce an obligation arising from liability under section 2 of the 1987 Act (to make reparation for damage caused wholly or partly by a defect in a product) where a person has died from personal injuries and the damages claimed include damages for those personal injuries or that death.

(2) Subject to subsection (4) below, an action to which this section applies shall not be competent unless it is commenced within the period of three years after the later of—

(a) the date of death of the injured person;

(b) the earliest date on which the person seeking to make (or a person who could at an earlier date have made) the claim was aware, or on which, in the opinion of the court, it was reasonably practicable for him in all the circumstances to become aware—

    (i)   that there was a defect in the product;

    (ii)   that the injuries of the deceased were caused (or partly caused) by the defect; and

    (iii)   that the defender was a person liable for the damage under the said section 2.

(3)   Where the person seeking to make the claim is a relative of the deceased, there shall be disregarded in the computation of the period mentioned in subsection (2) above any period during which that relative was under legal disability by reason of nonage or unsoundness of mind.

(4)   Where an action to which section 22B of this Act applies has not been brought within the period mentioned in subsection (2) of that section and the person subsequently dies in consequence of his injuries, an action to which this section applies shall not be competent in respect of those injuries or that death.

(5)   Where a person would be entitled, but for this section, to bring an action for reparation other than one in which the damages claimed are confined to damages for loss of or damage to property, the court may, if it seems to it equitable to do so, allow him to bring the action notwithstanding this section.

(6)   In this section 'relative' has the same meaning as in the Damages (Scotland) Act 1976.

(7)   For the purposes of subsection (2)(b) above there shall be disregarded knowledge of whether particular facts and circumstances would or would not, as a matter of law, result in liability for damage under the said section 2.

Supplementary

Interpretation of this Part

22D.—(1)   Expressions used in this Part and in Part I of the 1987 Act shall have the same meanings in this Part as in the said Part I.

(2)   For the purposes of section 1(1) of the 1987 Act, this Part shall have effect and be construed as if it were contained in Part I of that Act.

(3)   In this Part, "the 1987 Act" means the Consumer Protection Act 1987.'

11. Section 23 shall cease to have effect, but for the avoidance of doubt it is declared that the amendments in Part II of Schedule 4 shall continue to have effect.

12.   In paragraph 2 of Schedule 1, after subparagraph (gg) there shall be inserted the following subparagraph—

'(ggg)   to any obligation arising from liability under section 2 of the Consumer Protection Act 1987 (to make reparation for damage caused wholly or partly by a defect in a product);'.

Schedule 2   Prohibition Notices and Notices to Warn

Part I   Prohibition notices

1. A prohibition notice in respect of any goods shall—

(a)   state that the Secretary of State considers that the goods are unsafe;

(b)   set out the reasons why the Secretary of State considers that the goods are unsafe;

(c)   specify the day on which the notice is to come into force; and

(d)   state that the trader may at any time make representations in writing to the Secretary of State for the purpose of establishing that the goods are safe.

2.—(1)   If representations in writing about a prohibition notice are made by the trader to the Secretary of State, it shall be the duty of the Secretary of State to consider whether to revoke the notice and—

(a)   if he decides to revoke it, to do so;

(b)   in any other case, to appoint a person to consider those representations, any further representations made (whether in writing or orally) by the trader about the notice and the statements of any witnesses examined under this Part of this Schedule.

(2)   Where the Secretary of State has appointed a person to consider representations about a prohibition notice, he shall serve a notification on the trader which—

(a)   states that the trader may make oral representations to the appointed person for the purpose of establishing that the goods to which the notice relates are safe; and

(b)   specifies the place and time at which the oral representations may be made.

(3)   The time specified in a notification served under subparagraph (2) above shall not be before the end of the period of 21 days beginning with the day on which the notification is served, unless the trader otherwise agrees.

(4)   A person on whom a notification has been served under subparagraph (2) above or his representative may, at the place and time specified in the notification—

(a)   make oral representations to the appointed person for the purpose of establishing that the goods in question are safe; and

(b)   call and examine witnesses in connection with the representations.

3.—(1)   Where representations in writing about a prohibition notice are made by the trader to the Secretary of State at any time after a person has been appointed to consider representations about that notice, then, whether or not the appointed person has made a report to the Secretary of State, the following provisions of this paragraph shall apply instead of paragraph 2 above.

(2)   The Secretary of State shall, before the end of the period of one month beginning with the day on which he receives the representations, serve a notification on the trader which states—

(a)   that the Secretary of State has decided to revoke the notice, has decided to vary it or, as the case may be, has decided neither to revoke nor to vary it; or

(b)   that, a person having been appointed to consider representations about the notice, the trader may, at a place and time specified in the notification, make oral representations to the appointed person for the purpose of establishing that the goods to which the notice relates are safe.

(3)   The time specified in a notification served for the purposes of subparagraph (2)(b) above shall not be before the end of the period of 21 days beginning with the day on which the notification is served, unless the trader otherwise agrees or the time is the time already specified for the purposes of paragraph 2(2)(b) above.

(4)   A person on whom a notification has been served for the purposes of subparagraph (2)(b) above or his representative may, at the place and time specified in the notification—

(a)   make oral representations to the appointed person for the purpose of establishing that the goods in question are safe; and

(b)   call and examine witnesses in connection with the representations.

4.—(1)   Where a person is appointed to consider representations about a prohibition notice, it shall be his duty to consider—

(a)   any written representations made by the trader about the notice, other than those in respect of which a notification is served under paragraph 3(2)(a) above;

(b)   any oral representations made under paragraph 2(4) or 3(4) above; and

(c)   any statements made by witnesses in connection with the oral representations,

and, after considering any matters under this paragraph, to make a report (including recommendations) to the Secretary of State about the matters considered by him and the notice.

(2)   It shall be the duty of the Secretary of State to consider any report made to him under subparagraph (1) above and, after considering the report, to inform the trader of his decision with respect to the prohibition notice to which the report relates.

5.—(1)   The Secretary of State may revoke or vary a prohibition notice by serving on the trader a notification stating that the notice is revoked or, as the case may be, is varied as specified in the notification.

(2)   The Secretary of State shall not vary a prohibition notice so as to make the effect of the notice more restrictive for the trader.

(3)   Without prejudice to the power conferred by section 13(2) of this Act, the service of a notification under subparagraph (1) above shall be sufficient to satisfy the requirement of paragraph 4(2) above that the trader shall be informed of the Secretary of State's decision.

Part II   Notices to warn

6.—(1)   If the Secretary of State proposes to serve a notice to warn on any person in respect of any goods, the Secretary of State, before he serves the notice, shall serve on that person a notification which—

(a)   contains a draft of the proposed notice;

(b)   states that the Secretary of State proposes to serve a notice in the form of the draft on that person;

(c)   states that the Secretary of State considers that the goods described in the draft are unsafe;

(d)   sets out the reasons why the Secretary of State considers that those goods are unsafe; and

(e)   states that that person may make representations to the Secretary of State for the purpose of establishing that the goods are safe if, before the end of the period of 14 days beginning with the day on which the notification is served, he informs the Secretary of State—

(i)   of his intention to make representations; and

(ii)   whether the representations will be made only in writing or both in writing and orally.

(2)   Where the Secretary of State has served a notification containing a draft of a proposed notice to warn on any person, he shall not serve a notice to warn on that person in respect of the goods to which the proposed notice relates unless—

(a)   the period of 14 days beginning with the day on which the notification was served expires without the Secretary of State being informed as mentioned in subparagraph (1)(e) above;

(b)   the period of 28 days beginning with that day expires without any written representations being made by that person to the Secretary of State about the proposed notice; or

(c)   the Secretary of State has considered a report about the proposed notice by a person appointed under paragraph 7(1) below.

7.—(1)   Where a person on whom a notification containing a draft of a proposed notice to warn has been served—

(a)   informs the Secretary of State as mentioned in paragraph 6(1)(e) above before the end of the period of 14 days beginning with the day on which the notification was served; and

(b)   makes written representations to the Secretary of State about the proposed notice before the end of the period of 28 days beginning with that day,

the Secretary of State shall appoint a person to consider those representations, any further representations made by that person about the draft notice and the statements of any witnesses examined under this Part of this Schedule.

(2)   Where—

(a)   the Secretary of State has appointed a person to consider representations about a proposed notice to warn; and

(b)   the person whose representations are to be considered has informed the Secretary of State for the purposes of paragraph 6(1)(e) above that the representations he intends to make will include oral representations,

the Secretary of State shall inform the person intending to make the representations of the place and time at which oral representations may be made to the appointed person.

(3)   Where a person on whom a notification containing a draft of a proposed notice to warn has been served is informed of a time for the purposes of sub-paragraph (2) above, that time shall not be—

(a)   before the end of the period of 28 days beginning with the day on which the notification was served; or

(b)   before the end of the period of seven days beginning with the day on which that person is informed of the time.

(4)   A person who has been informed of a place and time for the purposes of subparagraph (2) above or his representative may, at that place and time—

(a)   make oral representations to the appointed person for the purpose of establishing that the goods to which the proposed notice relates are safe; and

(b)   call and examine witnesses in connection with the representations.

8.—(1)   Where a person is appointed to consider representations about a proposed notice to warn, it shall be his duty to consider—

(a)   any written representations made by the person on whom it is proposed to serve the notice; and

(b)   in a case where a place and time has been appointed under paragraph 7(2) above for oral representations to be made by that person or his representative, any representations so made and any statements made by witnesses in connection with those representations,

and, after considering those matters, to make a report (including recommendations) to the Secretary of State about the matters considered by him and the proposal to serve the notice.

(2)   It shall be the duty of the Secretary of State to consider any report made to him under subparagraph (1) above and, after considering the report, to inform the person on whom it was proposed that a notice to warn should be served of his decision with respect to the proposal.

(3)   If at any time after serving a notification on a person under paragraph 6 above the Secretary of State decides not to serve on that person either the proposed notice to warn or that notice with modifications, the Secretary of State shall inform that person of the decision; and nothing done for the purposes of any of the preceding provisions of this Part of this Schedule before that person was so informed shall—

(a)   entitle the Secretary of State subsequently to serve the proposed notice or that notice with modifications; or

(b)   require the Secretary of State, or any person appointed to consider representations about the proposed notice, subsequently to do anything in respect of, or in consequence of, any such representations.

(4)   Where a notification containing a draft of a proposed notice to warn is served on a person in respect of any goods, a notice to warn served on him in consequence of a decision made under subparagraph (2) above shall either be in the form of the draft or shall be less onerous than the draft.

9.   The Secretary of State may revoke a notice to warn by serving on the person on whom the notice was served a notification stating that the notice is revoked.

Part III   General

10.—(1)   Where a notification served on any person under this Schedule the Secretary of State has appointed a time for the making of oral representations or the examination of witnesses, he may, by giving that person such notification as the Secretary of State considers appropriate, change that time to a later time or appoint further times at which further representations may be made or the examination of witnesses may be continued; and paragraphs 2(4), 3(4) and 7(4) above shall have effect accordingly.

(2)   For the purposes of this Schedule the Secretary of State may appoint a person (instead of the appointed person) to consider any representations or statements, if the person originally appointed, or last appointed under this subparagraph, to consider those representations or statements has died or appears to the Secretary of State to be otherwise unable to act.

11.   In this Schedule—

'the appointed person' in relation to a prohibition notice or a proposal to serve a notice to warn, means the person for the time being appointed under this Schedule to consider representations about the notice or, as the case may be, about the proposed notice;

'notification' means a notification in writing;

'trader', in relation to a prohibition notice, means the person on whom the notice is or was served.

Schedule 3   Amendments of Part I of the Health and Safety at Work etc. Act 1974

1.—(1)   Section 6 (general duties of manufacturers etc. as regard articles and substances for use at work) shall be amended as follows.

(2)   For subsection (1) (general duties of designers, manufacturers, importers and suppliers of articles for use at work) there shall be substituted the following subsections—

'(1)   It shall be the duty of any person who designs, manufactures, imports or supplies any article for use at work or any article of fairground equipment—

(a)   to ensure, so far as is reasonably practicable, that the article is so designed and constructed that it will be safe and without risks to health at all times when it is being set, used, cleaned or maintained by a person at work;

(b)   to carry out or arrange for the carrying out of such testing and examination as may be necessary for the performance of the duty imposed on him by the preceding paragraph;

(c)   to take such steps as are necessary to secure that persons supplied by that person with the article are provided with adequate information about the use for which the article is designed or has been tested and about any conditions necessary to ensure that it will be safe and without risks to health at all such times as are mentioned in paragraph (a) above and when it is being dismantled or disposed of; and

(d)   to take such steps as are necessary to secure, so far as is reasonably practicable, that persons so supplied are provided with all such revisions of information provided to them by virtue of the preceding paragraph as are necessary by reason of its becoming known that anything gives rise to a serious risk to health or safety.

(1A)   It shall be the duty of any person who designs, manufactures, imports or supplies any article of fairground equipment—

(a) to ensure, so far as is reasonably practicable, that the article is so designed and constructed that it will be safe and without risks to health at all times when it is being used for or in connection with the entertainment of members of the public;

(b) to carry out or arrange for the carrying out of such testing and examination as may be necessary for the performance of the duty imposed on him by the preceding paragraph;

(c) to take such steps as are necessary to secure that persons supplied by that person with the article are provided with adequate information about the use for which the article is designed or has been tested and about any conditions necessary to ensure that it will be safe and without risks to health at all times when it is being used for or in connection with the entertainment of members of the public; and

(d) to take such steps as are necessary to secure, so far as is reasonably practicable, that persons so supplied are provided with all such revisions of information provided to them by virtue of the preceding paragraph as are necessary by reason of its becoming known that anything gives rise to a serious risk to health or safety.'

(3) In subsection (2) (duty of person who undertakes the design or manufacture of an article for use at work to carry out research), after the word 'work' there shall be inserted the words 'or of any article of fairground equipment'.

(4) In subsection (3) (duty of persons who erect or install articles for use at work)—

(a) after the words 'persons at work' there shall be inserted the words 'or who erects or installs any article of fairground equipment'; and

(b) for the words from 'it is' onwards there shall be substituted the words 'the article is erected or installed makes it unsafe or a risk to health at any such time as is mentioned in paragraph (a) of subsection (1) or, as the case may be, in paragraph (a) of subsection (1) or (1A) above.'

(5) For subsection (4) (general duties of manufacturers, importers and suppliers of substances for use at work) there shall be substituted the following subsection—

'(4) It shall be the duty of any person who manufactures, imports or supplies any substance—

(a) to ensure, so far as is reasonably practicable, that the substance will be safe and without risks to health at all times when it is being used, handled, processed, stored or transported by a person at work or in premises to which section 4 above applies;

(b) to carry out or arrange for the carrying out of such testing and examination as may be necessary for the performance of the duty imposed on him by the preceding paragraph;

(c) to take such steps as are necessary to secure that persons supplied by that person with the substance are provided with adequate information about any risks to health or safety to which the inherent properties of the substance may give rise, about the results of any relevant tests which have been carried out on or in connection with the substance and about any conditions necessary to ensure that the substance will be safe and without risks to health at all such times as are mentioned in paragraph (a) above and when the substance is being disposed of; and

(d) to take such steps as are necessary to secure, so far as is reasonably practicable, that persons so supplied are provided with all such revisions of information provided to them by virtue of the preceding paragraph as are necessary by reason of its becoming known that anything gives rise to a serious risk to health or safety.

(6) In subsection (5) (duty of person who undertakes the manufacture of a substance for use at work to carry out research)—

    (a) for the words 'substance for use at work' there shall be substituted the word 'substance'; and

    (b) at the end there shall be inserted the words 'at all such times as are mentioned in paragraph (a) of subsection (4) above'.

(7) In subsection (8) (relief from duties for persons relying on undertakings by others)—

    (a) for the words 'for or to another' there shall be substituted the words 'for use at work or an article of fairground equipment and does so for or to another';

    (b) for the words 'when properly used' there shall be substituted the words 'at all such times as are mentioned in paragraph (a) of subsection (1) or, as the case may be, in paragraph (a) of subsection (1) or (1A) above'; and

    (c) for the words 'by subsection (1)(a) above' there shall be substituted the words 'by virtue of that paragraph'.

(8) After the said subsection (8) there shall be inserted the following subsection—

    '(8A) Nothing in subsection (7) or (8) above shall relieve any person who imports any article or substance from any duty in respect of anything which—

    (a) in the case of an article designed outside the United Kingdom, was done by and in the course of any trade, profession or other undertaking carried on by, or was within the control of, the person who designed the article; or

    (b) in the case of an article or substance manufactured outside the United Kingdom, was done by and in the course of any trade, profession or other undertaking carried on by, or was within the control of, the person who manufactured the article or substance.'

(9) In subsection (9) (definition of supplier in certain cases of supply under a hire-purchase agreement), for the words 'article for use at work or substance for use at work' there shall be substituted the words 'article or substance'.

(10) For subsection (10) (meaning of 'properly used') there shall be substituted the following subsection—

    '(10) For the purposes of this section an absence of safety or a risk to health shall be disregarded in so far as the case in or in relation to which it would arise is shown to be one the occurrence of which could not reasonably be foreseen; and in determining whether any duty imposed by virtue of paragraph (a) of subsection (1), (1A) or (4) above has been performed regard shall be had to any relevant information or advice which has been provided to any person by the person by whom the article has been designed, manufactured, imported or supplied or, as the case may be, by the person by whom the substance has been manufactured, imported or supplied.'

2.   In section 22 (prohibition notices)—

(a)   in subsections (1) and (2) (notices in respect of activities which are or are about to be carried on and involve a risk of serious personal injury), for the word 'about', in each place where it occurs, there shall be substituted the word 'likely';

(b)   for subsection (4) (notice to have immediate effect only if the risk is imminent) there shall be substituted the following subsection—

'(4)   A direction contained in a prohibition notice in pursuance of subsection (3)(d) above shall take effect—

(a)   at the end of the period specified in the notice; or
(b)   if the notice so declares, immediately.'

3.   After section 25 there shall be inserted the following section—

Power of customs officer to detain articles and substances

25A.—(1)   A customs officer may, for the purpose of facilitating the exercise or performance by any enforcing authority or inspector of any of the powers or duties of the authority or inspector under any of the relevant statutory provisions, seize any imported article or imported substance and detain it for not more than two working days.

(2)   Anything seized and detained under this section shall be dealt with during the period of its detention in such manner as the Commissioners of Customs and Excise may direct.

(3)   In subsection (1) above the reference to two working days is a reference to a period of 48 hours calculated from the time when the goods in question are seized but disregarding so much of any period as falls on a Saturday or Sunday or on Christmas Day, Good Friday or a day which is a bank holiday under the Banking and Financial Dealings Act 1971 in the part of Great Britain where the goods are seized.'

4. After section 27 (power to obtain information) there shall be inserted the following section—

Information communicated by the Commissioners of Customs and Excise
27A.—(1)   If they think it appropriate to do so for the purpose of facilitating the exercise or performance by any person to whom subsection (2) below applies of any of that person's powers or duties under any of the relevant statutory provisions, the Commissioners of Customs and Excise may authorise the disclosure to that person of any information obtained for the purposes of the exercise by the Commissioners of their functions in relation to imports.

(2)   This subsection applies to an enforcing authority and to an inspector.

(3)   A disclosure of information made to any person under subsection (1) above shall be made in such manner as may be directed by the Commissioners of Customs and Excise and may be made through such persons acting on behalf of that person as may be so directed.

(4)   Information may be disclosed to a person under subsection (1) above whether or not the disclosure of the information has been requested by or on behalf of that person.'

5.   In section 28 (restrictions on disclosure of information), in subsection (1)(a), after the words 'furnished to any person' there shall be inserted the words 'under section 27A above or'.

6.   In section 33(1)(h) (offence of obstructing an inspector), after the word 'duties' there shall be inserted the words 'or to obstruct a customs officer in the exercise of his powers under section 25A'.

7.   In section 53(1) (general interpretation of Part I)—

(a)   after the definition of 'article for use at work' there shall be inserted the following definition—

' "article of fairground equipment" means any fairground equipment or any article designed for use as a component in any such equipment;'

(b)   after the definition of 'credit sale agreement' there shall be inserted the following definition—

' "customs officer" means an officer within the meaning of the Customs and Excise Management Act 1979;'

(c)   before the definition of 'the general purposes of this Part' there shall be inserted the following definition—

' "fairground equipment" means any fairground ride, any similar plant which is designed to be in motion for entertainment purposes with members of the public on or inside it or any plant which is designed to be used by members of the public for entertainment purposes either as a slide or for bouncing upon, and in this definition the reference to plant which is designed to be in motion with members of the public on or inside it includes a reference to swings, dodgems and other plant which is designed to be in motion wholly or partly under the control of, or to be put in motion by, a member of the public;'

(d)   after the definition of 'local authority' there shall be inserted the following definition—

' "micro-organism" includes any microscopic biological entity which is capable of replication;

(e)   in the definition of 'substance', after the words 'natural or artificial substance' there shall be inserted the words '(including micro-organisms)'.

Schedule 4   Minor and Consequential Amendments

The Explosives Act 1875

1.   In sections 31 and 80 of the Explosives Act 1875 (prohibitions on selling gunpowder to children and on use of fireworks in public places), for the words from 'shall be liable' onwards there shall be substituted the words 'shall be guilty of an offence and liable on summary conviction to a fine not exceeding level 5 on the standard scale'.

The Trade Descriptions Act 1968

2.—(1) In section 2 of the Trade Descriptions Act 1968 (meaning of trade description)—

(a) for paragraph (g) of subsection (4) (marks and descriptions applied in pursuance of the Consumer Safety Act 1978) there shall be substituted the following paragraph—

'(g) the Consumer Protection Act 1987;' and

(b) in subsection (5)(a) (descriptions prohibited under certain enactments), for the words 'or the Consumer Safety Act 1978' there shall be substituted the words 'or the Consumer Protection Act 1987'.

(2) In section 28(5A) of the said Act of 1968 (disclosure of information authorised for purpose specified in section 174(3) of the Consumer Credit Act 1974), for the words from 'section 174(3)' onwards there shall be substituted the words 'section 38(2)(a), (b) or (c) of the Consumer Protection Act 1987'.

The Fair Trading Act 1973

3. In section 130(1) of the Fair Trading Act 1973 (notice of intended prosecution by weights and measures authority to Director General of Fair Trading), after the words 'that Act,' there shall be inserted the words 'or for an offence under any provision made by or under Part III of the Consumer Protection Act 1987'.

The Consumer Credit Act 1974

4. In section 174(3)(a) of the Consumer Credit Act 1974 (exceptions to general restrictions on disclosure of information), after the words 'or the Airports Act 1986' there shall be inserted the words 'or the Consumer Protection Act 1987'.

The Torts (Interference with Goods) Act 1977

5. In section 1 of the Torts (Interference with Goods) Act 1977 (meaning of 'wrongful interference'), after paragraph (d) there shall be inserted the following words—

'and references in this Act (however worded) to proceedings for wrongful interference or to a claim or right to claim for wrongful interference shall include references to proceedings by virtue of Part I of the Consumer Protection Act 1987 (product liability) in respect of any damage to goods or to an interest in goods or, as the case may be, to a claim or right to claim by virtue of that Part in respect of any such damage.'

The Estate Agents Act 1979

6. In section 10(3)(a) of the Estate Agents Act 1979 (exceptions to general restrictions on disclosure of information), after the words 'or the Airports Act 1986' there shall be inserted the words 'or the Consumer Protection Act 1987'.

The Competition Act 1980

7.   In section 19(3) of the Competition Act 1980 (enactments specified in exceptions to general restrictions on disclosure of information), after paragraph (i) there shall be inserted the following paragraph—

   '(j)   the Consumer Protection Act 1987.'

The Employment Act 1982

8.   In section 16(2) of the Employment Act 1982 (proceedings against trade unions in relation to which the appropriate limit does not apply), after paragraph (b) there shall be inserted the following words—

   'or to any proceedings by virtue of Part I of the Consumer Protection Act 1987 (product liability).'

The Telecommunications Act 1984

9.—(1)   In sections 28(6) and 85(5)(b) of the Telecommunications Act 1984 (meaning of 'supply'), for the words 'be construed in accordance with section 9 of the Consumer Safety Act 1978' there shall be substituted the words 'have the same meaning as it has in Part II of the Consumer Protection Act 1987'.

   (2)   In section 101(3) of the said Act of 1984 (enactments specified in exceptions to general restrictions on disclosure of information), after paragraph (g) there shall be inserted the following paragraph—

   '(h)   the Consumer Protection Act 1987.'

The Airports Act 1986

10.   In section 74(3) of the Airports Act 1986 (enactments specified in exceptions to general restrictions on disclosure of information), after paragraph (h) there shall be inserted the following paragraph—

   '(i)   the Consumer Protection Act 1987.'

The Gas Act 1986

11.   In section 42 of the Gas Act 1986—

   (a)   in subsection (3) (restrictions on disclosure of information except for the purposes of certain enactments), at the end there shall be inserted the following paragraph—

   '(j)   the Consumer Protection Act 1987.';

   (b)   after subsection (5) there shall be inserted the following subsection—

   '(6)   In relation to the Consumer Protection Act 1987 the reference in subsection (2)(b) above to a weights and measures authority shall include a reference to any person on whom functions under that Act are conferred by regulation under section 27(2) of that Act.'

The Insolvency Act 1986

12.   In section 281(5)(a) of the Insolvency Act 1986 (discharge from bankruptcy not to release bankrupt from liability in respect of personal injuries), for the word 'being' there shall be substituted the words 'or to pay damages by virtue of Part I of the Consumer Protection Act 1987, being in either case'.

The Motor Cycle Noise Act 1987

13.   For paragraphs 3 to 5 of the Schedule to the Motor Cycle Noise Act 1987 (enforcement) there shall be substituted the following paragraph—

'3.   Part IV of the Consumer Protection Act 1987 (enforcement), except section 31 (power of customs officers to detain goods), shall have effect as if the provisions of this Act were safety provisions within the meaning of that Act; and in Part V of that Act (miscellaneous and supplemental), except in section 49 (Northern Ireland), references to provision of the said Part IV shall include references to those provisions as applied by this paragraph.'.

Schedule 5   Repeals

Chapter	Short title	Extent of repeal
3 & 4 Geo. 5. c. 17.	The Fabrics (Misdescription) Act 1913.	The whole Act.
1967 c. 80.	The Criminal Justice Act 1967.	In Part I of Schedule 3, the entry relating to the Fabrics (Misdescription) Act 1913.
1967 c. 29. (N.I.).	The Fines Act (Northern Ireland) 1967.	In Part I of the Schedule, the entry relating to the Fabrics (Misdescription) Act 1913.
1968 c. 29.	The Trade Descriptions Act 1968.	Section 11.
1972 c. 34.	The Trade Descriptions Act 1972.	The whole Act.
1972 c. 70.	The Local Government Act 1972.	In Part II of Schedule 29, paragraph 18(1).

1973 c. 52.	The Prescription and Limitation (Scotland) Act 1973.	Section 23.
1973 c. 65.	The Local Government (Scotland) Act 1973.	In Part II of Schedule 27, paragraph 50.
1974 c. 37	The Health and Safety at Work etc. Act 1974.	In section 53(1), the definition of 'substance for use at work'.
1976 c. 26.	The Explosives (Age of Purchase etc.) Act 1976.	In section 1, in subsection (1), the words from 'and for the word' onwards and subsection (2).
1978 c. 38.	The Consumer Safety Act 1978.	The whole Act.
1980 c. 43.	The Magistrates' Courts Act 1980.	In Schedule 7, paragraphs 172 and 173.
1984 c. 12.	The Telecommunications Act 1984.	In section 101(3)(f), the word 'and'.
1984 c. 30.	The Food Act 1984.	In Schedule 10, paragraph 32.
1986 c. 29.	The Consumer Safety (Amendment) Act 1986.	The whole Act.
1986 c. 31.	The Airports Act 1986.	In section 74(3)(g), the word 'and'.
1986 c. 44.	The Gas Act 1986.	In section 42(3), paragraphs (a) and (g) and, in paragraph (h), the word 'and'.

The Product Liability Directive

Council directive of 25 July 1985 on the approximation of the laws, regulations and administrative provisions of the Member States concerning liability for defective products (85/374/EEC).

THE COUNCIL OF THE EUROPEAN COMMUNITIES,

Having regard to the Treaty establishing the European Economic Community, and in particular Article 100 thereof,

Having regard to the proposal from the Commission [OJ No. C 241, 14 October 1976, p.9 and OJ No. C 271, 26 October 1979, p.3],

Having regard to the opinion of the European Parliament [OJ No. C 127, 21 May 1979, p.61]

Having regard to the opinion of the Economic and Social Committee [OJ No. C 114, 7 May 1979, p.15],

Whereas approximation of the laws of the Member States concerning the liability of the producer for damage caused by the defectiveness of his products is necessary because the existing divergences may distort competition and affect the movement of goods within the common market and entail a differing degree of protection of the consumer against damage caused by a defective product to his health or property;

Whereas liability without fault on the part of the producer is the sole means of adequately solving the problem, peculiar to our age of increasing technicality, of a fair apportionment of the risks inherent in modern technological production;

Whereas liability without fault should apply only to movables which have been industrially produced; whereas, as a result, it is appropriate to exclude liability for agricultural products and game, except where they have undergone a processing of an industrial nature which could cause a defect in these products; whereas the liability provided for in this Directive should also apply to movables which are used in the construction of immovables or are installed in immovables;

Whereas protection of the consumer requires that all producers involved in the production process should be made liable, in so far as their finished product, component part or any raw material supplied by them was defective; whereas, for the same reason, liability should extend to importers of products into the Community and to persons who present themselves as producers by affixing their name, trade mark or other distinguishing feature or who supply a product the producer of which cannot be identified;

Whereas, in situations where several persons are liable for the same damage, the protection of the consumer requires that the injured person should be able to claim full compensation for the damage from any one of them;

Whereas, to protect the physical well-being and property of the consumer, the defectiveness of the product should be determined by reference not to its fitness for use but to the lack of the safety which the public at large is entitled to expert; whereas the safety is assessed by excluding any misuse of the product not reasonable under the circumstances;

Whereas a fair apportionment of risk between the injured person and the producer implies that the producer should be able to free himself from liability if he furnishes proof as to the existence of certain exonerating circumstances;

Whereas the protection of the consumer requires that the liability of the producer remains unaffected by acts or omissions of other persons having contributed to cause the damage; whereas, however, the contributory negligence of the injured person may be taken into account to reduce or disallow such liability;

Whereas the protection of the consumer requires compensation for death and personal injury as well as compensation for damage to property; whereas the latter should nevertheless be limited to goods for private use or consumption and be subject to a deduction of a lower threshold of a fixed amount in order to avoid litigation in an excessive number of cases; whereas this Directive should not prejudice compensation for pain and suffering and other non-material damages payable, where appropriate, under the law applicable to the case;

Whereas a uniform period of limitation for the bringing of action for compensation is in the interests both of the injured person and of the producer;

Whereas products age in the course of time, higher safety standards are developed and the state of science and technology progresses; whereas, therefore, it would not be reasonable to make the producer liable for an unlimited period for the defectiveness of his product; whereas, therefore, liability should expire after a reasonable length of time, without prejudice to claims pending at law;

Whereas, to achieve effective protection of consumers, no contractual derogation should be permitted as regards the liability of the producer in relation to the injured person;

Whereas under the legal systems of the Member States an injured party may have a claim for damages based on grounds of contractual liability or on grounds of non-contractual liability other than that provided for in this Directive; in so far as these provisions also serve to attain the objective of effective protection of consumers, they should remain unaffected by this Directive; whereas, in so far as effective protection of consumers in the sector of pharmaceutical products is already also attained in a Member State under a special liability system, claims based on this system should similarly remain possible;

Whereas, to the extent that liability for nuclear injury or damage is already covered in all Member States by adequate special rules, it has been possible to exclude damage of this type from the scope of this Directive;

Whereas, since the exclusion of primary agricultural products and game from the scope of this Directive may be felt, in certain Member States, in view of what is expected for the protection of consumers, to restrict unduly such protection, it should be possible for a Member State to extend liability to such products;

Whereas, for similar reasons, the possibility offered to a producer to free himself from liability if he proves that the state of scientific and technical knowledge at the time when he put the product into circulation was not such as to enable the existence of a defect to be discovered may be felt in certain Member States to restrict unduly the protection of the consumer; whereas it should therefore be possible for a Member State to maintain in its legislation or to provide by new legislation that this exonerating circumstance is not admitted; whereas, in the case of new legislation, making use of this derogation should, however, be subject to a Community stand-still procedure, in order to raise, if possible, the level of protection in a uniform manner throughout the Community;

Whereas, taking into account the legal traditions in most of the Member States, it is inappropriate to set any financial ceiling on the producer's liability without fault; whereas, in so far as there are, however, differing traditions, it seems possible to admit that a Member State may derogate from the principle of unlimited liability by providing a limit for the total liability of the producer for damage resulting from a death or personal injury and caused by identical items with the same defect, provided that this limit is established at a level sufficiently high to guarantee adequate protection of the consumer and the correct functioning of the common market;

Whereas the harmonization resulting from this cannot be total at the present stage, but opens the way towards greater harmonization; whereas it is therefore necessary that the Council receive at regular intervals, reports from the Commission on the application of this Directive, accompanied, as the case may be, by appropriate proposals;

Whereas it is particularly important in this respect that a re-examination be carried out of those parts of the Directive relating to the derogations open to the Member States, at the expiry of a period of sufficient length to gather practical experience on the effects of these derogations on the protection of consumers and on the functioning of the common market,

HAS ADOPTED THIS DIRECTIVE:

Article 1

The producer shall be liable for damage caused by a defect in his product.

Article 2

For the purpose of this Directive 'product' means all movables, with the exception of primary agricultural products and game, even though incorporated into another movable or into an immovable. 'Primary agricultural products' means the products of the soil, of stock-farming and of fisheries, excluding products which have undergone initial processing. 'Product' includes electricity.

Article 3

1.   'Producer' means the manufacturer of a finished product, the producer of any raw material or the manufacturer of a component part and any person who, by putting his name, trade mark or other distinguishing feature on the product presents himself as its producer.

2.   Without prejudice to the liability of the producer, any person who imports into the Community a product for sale, hire, leasing or any form of distribution in the course of his business shall be deemed to be a producer within the meaning of this Directive and shall be responsible as a producer.

3.   Where the producer of the product cannot be identified, each supplier of the product shall be treated as its producer unless he informs the injured person, within a reasonable time, of the identity of the producer or of the person who supplied him with the product. The same shall apply, in the case of an imported product, if this product does not indicate the identity of the importer referred to in paragraph 2, even if the name of the producer is indicated.

Article 4

The injured person shall be required to prove the damage, the defect and the causal relationship between defect and damage.

Article 5

Where, as a result of the provisions of this Directive, two or more persons are liable for the same damage, they shall be liable jointly and severally, without prejudice to the provisions of national law concerning the rights of contribution or recourse.

Article 6

1.   A product is defective when it does not provide the safety which a person is entitled to expect, taking all circumstances into account, including:

(a)   the presentation of the product;
(b)   the use to which it could reasonably be expected that the product would be put;
(c)   the time when the product was put into circulation.

2.   A product shall not be considered defective for the sole reason that a better product is subsequently put into circulation.

Article 7

The producer shall not be liable as result of this Directive if he proves:

(a)   that he did not put the product into circulation; or
(b)   that, having regard to the circumstances, it is probable that the defect which caused the damage did not exist at the time when the product was put into circulation by him or that this defect came into being afterwards; or
(c)   that the product was neither manufactured by him for sale or any form of distribution for economic purpose nor manufactured or distributed by him in the course of his business; or
(d)   that the defect is due to compliance of the product with mandatory regulations issued by the public authorities; or
(e)   that the state of scientific and technical knowledge at the time when he put the product into circulation was not such as to enable the existence of the defect to be discovered; or
(f)   in the case of a manufacturer of a component, that the defect is attributable to the design of the product in which the component has been fitted or to the instructions given by the manufacturer of the product.

Article 8

1.   Without prejudice to the provisions of national law concerning the right of contribution or recourse, the liability of the producer shall not be reduced when the damage is caused both by a defect in product and by the act or omission of a third party.

2.   The liability of the producer may be reduced or disallowed when, having regard to all the circumstances, the damage is caused both by a defect in the product and by the fault of the injured person or any person for whom the injured person is responsible.

Article 9

For the purpose of Article 1, 'damage' means:

  (a) damage caused by death or by personal injuries;

  (b) damage to, or destruction of, any item of property other than the defective product itself, with a lower threshold of 500 ECU, provided that the item of property:

    (i) is of a type ordinarily intended for private use or consumption, and

    (ii) was used by the injured person mainly for his own private use or consumption.

This Article shall be without prejudice to national provisions relating to non-material damage.

Article 10

1. Member States shall provide in their legislation that a limitation period of three years shall apply to proceedings for the recovery of damages as provided for in this Directive. The limitation period shall begin to run from the day on which the plaintiff became aware, or should reasonably have become aware, of the damage, the defect and the identity of the producer.

2. The laws of Member States regulating suspension or interruption of the limitation period shall not be affected by this Directive.

Article 11

Member States shall provide in their legislation that the rights conferred upon the injured person pursuant to this Directive shall be extinguished upon the expiry of a period of 10 years from the date on which the producer put into circulation the actual product which caused the damage, unless the injured person has in the meantime instituted proceedings against the producer.

Article 12

The liability of the producer arising from this Directive may not, in relation to the injured person, be limited or excluded by a provision limiting his liability or exempting him from liability.

Article 13

This Directive shall not affect any rights which an injured person may have according to the rules of the law of contractual or non-contractual liability or a special liability system existing at the moment when this Directive is notified.

Article 14

This Directive shall not apply to injury or damage arising from nuclear accidents and covered by international conventions ratified by the Member States.

Article 15

1. Each Member State may:

(a) by way of derogation from Article 2, provide in its legislation that within the meaning of Article 1 of this Directive 'product' also means primary agricultural products and game;

(b) by way of derogation from Article 7(e), maintain or, subject to the procedure set out in paragraph 2 of this Article, provide in this legislation that the producer shall be liable even if he proves that the state of scientific and technical knowledge at the time when he put the product into circulation was not such as to enable the existence of a defect to be discovered.

2. A Member State wishing to introduce the measure specified in paragraph 1(b) shall communicate the text of the proposed measure to the Commission. The Commission shall inform the other Member States thereof.

The Member State concerned shall hold the proposed measure in abeyance for nine months after the Commission is informed and provided that in the meantime the Commission has not submitted to the Council a proposal amending this Directive on the relevant matter. However, if within three months of receiving the said information, the Commission does not advise the Member State concerned that it intends submitting such a proposal to the Council, the Member State may take the proposed measure immediately.

If the Commission does submit to the Council such a proposal amending this Directive within the aforementioned nine months, the Member State concerned shall hold the proposed measure in abeyance for a further period of 18 months from the date on which the proposal is submitted.

3. Ten years after the date of notification of this Directive, the Commission shall submit to the Council a report on the effect that rulings by the courts as to the application of Article 7(e) and of paragraph 1(b) of this Article have on consumer protection and the functioning of the common market. In the light of this report the Council, acting on a proposal from the Commission and pursuant to the terms of Article 100 of the Treaty, shall decide whether to repeal Article 7(e).

Article 16

1. Any Member State may provide that a producer's total liability for damage resulting from a death or personal injury and caused by identical items with the same defect shall be limited to an amount which may not be less than 70 million ECU.

2. Ten years after the date of notification of this Directive, the Commission shall submit to the Council a report on the effect on consumer protection and the functioning of the common market of the implementation of the financial limit on liability by those Member States which have used the option provided for in paragraph 1. In the light of this report the Council, acting on a proposal from the Commission and pursuant to the terms of Article 100 of the Treaty, shall decide whether to repeal paragraph 1.

Article 17

This Directive shall not apply to products put into circulation before the date on which the provisions referred to in Article 19 enter into force.

Article 18

1. For the purposes of this Directive, the ECU shall be that defined by Regulation (EEC) No 3180/78 [OJ No. L 379, 30 December 1978, p.1], as amended by Regulation (EEC) No 2626/84 [OJ No. L 247, 16 September 1984, p.1]. The equivalent in national currency shall initially be calculated at the rate obtaining on the date of adoption of this Directive.

2. Every five years the Council, acting on a proposal from the Commission, shall examine and, if need be, revise the amounts in this Directive, in the light of economic and monetary trends in the Community.

Article 19

1. Member States shall bring into force, not later than three years from the date of notification of this Directive, the laws, regulations and administrative provisions necessary to comply with this Directive. They shall forthwith inform the Commission thereof [This Directive was notified to Member States on 30 July 1985.]

2. The procedure set out in Article 15(2) shall apply from the date of notification of this Directive.

Article 20

Member States shall communicate to the Commission the texts of the main provisions of national law which they subsequently adopt in the field governed by this Directive.

Article 21

Every five years the Commission shall present a report to the Council on the application of this Directive and, if necessary, shall submit appropriate proposals to it.

Article 22

This Directive is addressed to the Member States.

Done at Brussels, 25 July 1985.

For the Council

The President

J. POOS

Index